First World War
and Army of Occupation
War Diary
France, Belgium and Germany

49 DIVISION
Divisional Troops
Divisional Trench Mortar Batteries
9 July 1915 - 30 November 1918

WO95/2782/3

The Naval & Military Press Ltd
www.nmarchive.com
Published in association with The National Archives

Published by

The Naval & Military Press Ltd

Unit 10 Ridgewood Industrial Park,
Uckfield, East Sussex,
TN22 5QE England
Tel: +44 (0) 1825 749494

www.naval-military-press.com
www.nmarchive.com

This diary has been reprinted in facsimile from the original. Any imperfections are inevitably reproduced and the quality may fall short of modern type and cartographic standards.

© **Crown Copyright**
Images reproduced by permission of The National Archives, London, England, 2015.

Contents

Document type	Place/Title	Date From	Date To
Heading	BEF 49 Div Troops 39 Trench Mortar Bty 1915 Sept-1915 Nov		
War Diary		19/09/1915	22/10/1915
War Diary	Trenches	22/10/1915	31/10/1915
War Diary	Billets	31/10/1915	06/11/1915
War Diary	Poperinghe	07/11/1915	30/11/1915
Heading	49 Div 34 Trench Mortar Bty 1915 July to 1915 Dec.		
War Diary		09/07/1915	31/07/1915
War Diary	C.7.c.2.8.	08/08/1915	28/08/1915
War Diary		30/08/1915	04/09/1915
War Diary	In the field	12/09/1915	20/09/1915
War Diary	Map 1/20,000 Sheet 8 S.W. B.29.a.3.3.	21/09/1915	25/09/1915
War Diary	In the Field.	26/09/1915	30/10/1915
War Diary	In the Field.	28/11/1915	04/12/1915
War Diary	In the Field.	21/11/1915	27/11/1915
War Diary	In the field F31-35.	14/11/1915	20/11/1915
War Diary	In the field F31-F35.	07/11/1915	13/11/1915
War Diary	In the field	31/10/1915	31/10/1915
War Diary	Billet 1/20,000 S.28 N.W. B.29.A.3.3 Battery F31-35.	01/10/1915	06/10/1915
War Diary	In the field	12/12/1915	25/12/1915
War Diary	In the field F31-F35.	19/12/1915	01/01/1916
War Diary	In the field	17/09/1915	23/09/1915
War Diary	In the field	05/12/1915	11/12/1915
Heading	49th Division Divl Trench Mortar Battery 1915 Jly-1918 Dec		
Heading	War Diary of 49th Divl Trench Mortar Battery for December 1916.		
War Diary	France	01/12/1916	01/12/1916
War Diary	Henu.	01/12/1916	21/12/1916
War Diary	Halloy (Sheet 51c) 1/40,000.	22/12/1916	25/12/1916
War Diary	Halloy	26/12/1916	31/12/1916
Heading	War Diaries of 49th Divisional Trench Mortar Batteries for January 1917. Vol 2.		
War Diary	France Halloy	01/01/1917	10/01/1917
War Diary	Halloy	11/01/1917	21/01/1917
War Diary	France Bavincourt Berles & Crosville	22/01/1917	31/01/1917
Miscellaneous	Positions of Trench Mortar Emplacements 49th Division.		
Miscellaneous	Trench Mortar Positions 49th Division.		
Operation(al) Order(s)	Trench Mortar Operation Order No: 10/33.	28/01/1917	28/01/1917
Heading	War Diary of 49th (WR) Divl Trench Mortar Batteries for February 1917. Vol 3.		
War Diary	Bavincourt Berles & Grosville Reference maps Blaireville 51c S.E. 4. Edition 2 A. 1/10000. Figheux 51c S.E. Edition 2 C. 1/10000, France Sheet 57.c	01/02/1917	19/02/1917
War Diary	Wailly Bavincourt Berues & Grosville. Reference map Blaireville 51C S.E. 4. Edition 2 A. 1/10000 Ficheux 51c S.E. Edition 2c 1/10,000. France Sheet 51C.	20/02/1917	25/02/1917
War Diary	Berles Grosvilles & Bavincourt	26/02/1917	28/02/1917

Heading	War Diary of 49th Divisional Trench Mortar Batteries for March 1917.		
Heading	Grosville Berles Basseux Bavincourt Ref. maps (Lens II) 1/100,000.	01/03/1917	02/03/1917
War Diary	Ficheux 51c. S.E. & 51b.S.W. Edition 2 c. 1/10,000.	02/03/1917	03/03/1917
War Diary	Ransart 51c. S.E. 3&4 Edition 3.c.1/10,000.	03/03/1917	05/03/1917
War Diary	Doullens Reference map (Lens 11.) 1/100,000.	06/03/1917	06/03/1917
War Diary	Merville ref. map (Hazebrouk 5.A) 1/100,000.	07/03/1917	08/03/1917
War Diary	Lagorgue Ref. map. Hazebrouk 5 A. 1/100,000.	09/03/1917	09/03/1917
War Diary	Richebourg & Laventie (Reference maps)	10/03/1917	10/03/1917
War Diary	Richebourg 36.S.W.3. Edition 7c.1/10,000.& Aubers 36. S.W. 1 Edition 70 1/10,000.	11/03/1917	13/03/1917
War Diary	Laventie & Richebourg Ref Maps Richebourg 36 S.W. 3 Edition 7c 1/10,000 Aubers 36 S.W. 1 Edition 7c 1/10,000.	14/03/1917	31/03/1917
Heading	War Diary of 49th (WR) Divl Trench Mortar Battery April /17 Vol 5.		
War Diary	Laventie & Richebourg Ref Maps Richebourg 36 S.W. 3 Edition 8a 1/10,000 Aubers 36 S.W. 1 Edition 8a 1/10,000.	01/04/1917	30/04/1917
Heading	War Diary of 49th Div Trench Mortar Batteries for month of May 1917. Vol 6.		
War Diary	Laventie & Richebourg Ref Maps Richebourg 36 S.W. 3 Edition 8a 1/10,000 Aubers 36 S.W. 1 Edition 8a 1/10,000.	01/05/1917	31/05/1917
Heading	War Diary of 49th (WR) Divl Trench Mortar Batteries for June 1917. Vol 7.		
Heading	War Diary of 49th Div Trench Mortar Batteries for month of June 1917.		
War Diary	Laventie Ref Maps Richebourg 36 S.W. 3 Edition 8a 1/10,000 Aubers 36 S.W. 1 Edition 8a 1/10,000.	01/06/1917	30/06/1917
Heading	War Diary of 49th Div Trench Mortar for month of July 1917. Vol 8.		
War Diary	Laventie Ref Maps Richebourg 36 S.W. 3. Edition 8a 1/10,000 Aubers 36 S.W. 1 Edition 8a 1/10,000.	01/07/1917	09/07/1917
War Diary	Le. Sart. Ref. Map France Sheet 36 a Edition 6	10/07/1917	13/07/1917
War Diary	Leffring Koucke Ref Map Belgium & France Sheet 19 (Edition.2.)	14/07/1917	15/07/1917
War Diary	Teteghem map Ref. (I.15.a.80.00) Ref map:- Belgium & France Sheet 19.	16/07/1917	18/07/1917
War Diary	Coxyde Ref map. Oost-Dunkerke Sheet 11.	18/07/1917	22/07/1917
War Diary	Coxyde Ref Map Belgium Sheet 11 Nieuport. Ref. Map Nieuport 12.S.W. 1. Edition 2a.	23/07/1917	31/07/1917
Heading	War Diary of 49 Div T.M. Batteries for month of August 1917. Vol 9.		
War Diary	Coxyde Ref Map Belgium Sheet 11	01/08/1917	01/08/1917
War Diary	Nieuport Ref Map	01/08/1917	01/08/1917
War Diary	Nieuport 12 S.W. 1 Edition 2 A	02/08/1917	15/08/1917
War Diary	Coxyde Ref Map Belgium Sheet 11	16/08/1917	16/08/1917
War Diary	Nieuport 12 S.W. 1 Edition 2 A	17/08/1917	31/08/1917
Heading	49th Division Trench Mortar Batteries War Diary September 1917. Vol 10.		
War Diary	Coxyde	01/09/1917	08/09/1917
War Diary	Uxem	09/09/1917	09/09/1917
War Diary	Wormhoult	10/09/1917	11/09/1917
War Diary	Croix De Poperinghe Dranoutre	12/09/1917	27/09/1917

War Diary	Watou	28/09/1917	30/09/1917
Heading	War Diary of 49th Div Trench Mortar Batteries for month of October 1917. Vol 11.		
War Diary	Watou and near Gravenstafel	01/10/1917	31/10/1917
Heading	War Diary 49th Division Trench Mortar Batteries November 1917 Vol 12.		
War Diary	Watou Ypres.	01/11/1917	30/11/1917
War Diary		28/11/1917	28/11/1917
Heading	War Diary 49 Div Trench Mortar Batteries for the month of December 1917 Vol 13.		
War Diary	Ypres	01/12/1917	02/12/1917
War Diary	Vieux Berquin.	03/12/1917	31/12/1917
War Diary		20/12/1917	20/12/1917
Miscellaneous	49th Divl T.M. Batteries Programme of Training for Week-Ending 30.12.17.	30/12/1917	30/12/1917
Heading	War Diary of B.T.M.O. 49 Div for month of January 1918 Vol 14.		
War Diary	Vieux Berquin	01/01/1918	04/01/1918
War Diary	Noordpeene	05/01/1918	31/01/1918
Heading	War Diary 49 Div Trench Mortar Batteries February 1918. Vol 15.		
War Diary	Noordpeene	01/02/1918	21/02/1918
War Diary	Kruistraat	22/02/1918	23/02/1918
War Diary	Gheluvelt Sector.	23/02/1918	28/02/1918
Heading	War Diary 49th Trench Mortar Batteries March 1918. Vol 16.		
War Diary	Geluvelt Sector.	01/03/1918	31/03/1918
Heading	49th Divisional Artillery. 49th Divisional Trench Mortars April 1918.		
War Diary	Gheluvelt Sector.	01/04/1918	30/04/1918
Heading	War Diary of 49th Div Trench Mortar Batteries for month of May 1918. Vol 18.		
War Diary	Ypres Sector.	01/05/1918	31/05/1918
Heading	War Diary 49th Trench Mortar Batteries for month of June 1918. Vol 19.		
War Diary	Ypres Sector.	01/06/1918	30/06/1918
Heading	War Diary of 49th (WR) Division (Medium) Trench Mortar Batteries for July 1918. Vol 20.		
War Diary	Ypres Sector.	01/07/1918	31/07/1918
Heading	War Diary of 49th Division Medium Trench Mortar Batteries for August 1918. Vol 21.		
War Diary	Ypres Sector.	01/08/1918	04/08/1918
War Diary	Ypres Sector Ref Map Sheet 28 1/40,000.	05/08/1918	15/08/1918
War Diary	Ypres Sector	16/08/1918	21/08/1918
War Diary	Haandekot	21/08/1918	25/08/1918
War Diary	Ebblingham Ref Map Hazebrouck 5A 1/100,000.	26/08/1918	26/08/1918
War Diary	Amettes Ref Map Hazebrouck 5A 1/100,000	27/08/1918	27/08/1918
War Diary	Ramecourt Ref Map Lens 11 1/100,000	28/08/1918	31/08/1918
Heading	War Diary 49th Division Trench Mortar Batteries September 1918 Vol 22.		
War Diary	Ramecourt 2.D.80.40.	01/09/1918	01/09/1918
War Diary	Frevin Capelle Z.H.10.25.	02/09/1918	13/09/1918
War Diary	Billets at H.7.c.3.5. Ref map. Sheet 51b. and position in the line	14/09/1918	23/09/1918
War Diary	Bray Ref Map Sheet 51 c F.14.b.5.5.	24/09/1918	26/09/1918
War Diary	Bray	26/09/1918	30/09/1918

Heading	War Diary 49 Divisional Trench Mortar Batteries for the month of October 1918. Vol 23.		
War Diary	Reference map Lens 11 1/100,000.		
War Diary	Brandt Camp	01/10/1918	09/10/1918
War Diary	Lens 2.I.2.1.3	09/10/1918	09/10/1918
War Diary	Cherisy Lens 4.K.9.2.77	09/10/1918	09/10/1918
War Diary	Reference Valenciennes. 1/100,000	10/10/1918	10/10/1918
War Diary	Billelts 4.c.60.12	10/10/1918	10/10/1918
War Diary	Escadoeuvres 4.D.25.25	12/10/1918	12/10/1918
War Diary	Naves	23/10/1918	23/10/1918
War Diary	4.D.42.78.	25/10/1918	25/10/1918
War Diary	Billets at 3.E.77.8.4.	28/10/1918	31/10/1918
War Diary	Reference map Valenciennes 1/100,000 Billelts at 3.E.77.8.4.		
War Diary	Bilelts at 3.E.77.8.4	01/11/1918	05/11/1918
War Diary	Bilelts at 2.G.31.12 Nr Valemciennes	06/11/1918	09/11/1918
War Diary	Erquennes 2.J.51.31	10/11/1918	27/11/1918
War Diary	Marly 2.G.5.2	28/11/1918	28/11/1918
War Diary	Mastaing 3.D.65.61	29/11/1918	30/11/1918
War Diary	Reference map Valenciennes 1/100,000		

BEF

49 Div Troops

39

Trench Mortar Bty

1915 Sept - 1915 Nov

WAR DIARY or INTELLIGENCE SUMMARY

Army Form C. 2118

29th Div. H.Q. French Division Buffs

Place	Date	Hour	Summary of Events and Information	Remarks and references to Appendices
	19.9.15	7.30pm	Relieved Lieut. Benham. Fairly quiet during the night no firing by French stormers today.	
	20.9.15	5.0 am	Heavy bombardment on both sides by Artillery, during which our parapets were blown down completely at two [?] places. Keeping the gun's blanket [?] in dugouts where bombs were stored, spare parts kept. Considerable time was spent in digging out the gun's stores & turning the whole of our side took damages it was necessary to move ammunition stores & make part of the line. It was constant movement to fire this day we were. 7.2". battery keeping pieces hidden on position. The possibility of retaliation by enemy impressing the danger of such exposure for those guns, which were essential for impending attack. Bombardment by Artillery continued throughout the day but scarcely quiet during the night. Relief men & support in consequence heavy.	

War Diary	Watou	28/09/1917	30/09/1917
Heading	War Diary of 49th Div Trench Mortar Batteries for month of October 1917. Vol 11.		
War Diary	Watou and near Gravenstafel	01/10/1917	31/10/1917
Heading	War Diary 49th Division Trench Mortar Batteries November 1917 Vol 12.		
War Diary	Watou Ypres.	01/11/1917	30/11/1917
War Diary		28/11/1917	28/11/1917
Heading	War Diary 49 Div Trench Mortar Batteries for the month of December 1917 Vol 13.		
War Diary	Ypres	01/12/1917	02/12/1917
War Diary	Vieux Berquin.	03/12/1917	31/12/1917
War Diary		20/12/1917	20/12/1917
Miscellaneous	49th Divl T.M. Batteries Programme of Training for Week-Ending 30.12.17.	30/12/1917	30/12/1917
Heading	War Diary of B.T.M.O. 49 Div for month of January 1918 Vol 14.		
War Diary	Vieux Berquin	01/01/1918	04/01/1918
War Diary	Noordpeene	05/01/1918	31/01/1918
Heading	War Diary 49 Div Trench Mortar Batteries February 1918. Vol 15.		
War Diary	Noordpeene	01/02/1918	21/02/1918
War Diary	Kruistraat	22/02/1918	23/02/1918
War Diary	Gheluvelt Sector.	23/02/1918	28/02/1918
Heading	War Diary 49th Trench Mortar Batteries March 1918. Vol 16.		
War Diary	Geluvelt Sector.	01/03/1918	31/03/1918
Heading	49th Divisional Artillery. 49th Divisional Trench Mortars April 1918.		
War Diary	Gheluvelt Sector.	01/04/1918	30/04/1918
Heading	War Diary of 49th Div Trench Mortar Batteries for month of May 1918. Vol 18.		
War Diary	Ypres Sector.	01/05/1918	31/05/1918
Heading	War Diary 49th Trench Mortar Batteries for month of June 1918. Vol 19.		
War Diary	Ypres Sector.	01/06/1918	30/06/1918
Heading	War Diary of 49th (WR) Division (Medium) Trench Mortar Batteries for July 1918. Vol 20.		
War Diary	Ypres Sector.	01/07/1918	31/07/1918
Heading	War Diary of 49th Division Medium Trench Mortar Batteries for August 1918. Vol 21.		
War Diary	Ypres Sector.	01/08/1918	04/08/1918
War Diary	Ypres Sector Ref Map Sheet 28 1/40,000.	05/08/1918	15/08/1918
War Diary	Ypres Sector	16/08/1918	21/08/1918
War Diary	Haandekot	21/08/1918	25/08/1918
War Diary	Ebblingham Ref Map Hazebrouck 5A 1/100,000.	26/08/1918	26/08/1918
War Diary	Amettes Ref Map Hazebrouck 5A 1/100,000	27/08/1918	27/08/1918
War Diary	Ramecourt Ref Map Lens 11 1/100,000	28/08/1918	31/08/1918
Heading	War Diary 49th Division Trench Mortar Batteries September 1918 Vol 22.		
War Diary	Ramecourt 2.D.80.40.	01/09/1918	01/09/1918
War Diary	Frevin Capelle Z.H.10.25.	02/09/1918	13/09/1918
War Diary	Billets at H.7.c.3.5. Ref map. Sheet 51b. and position in the line	14/09/1918	23/09/1918
War Diary	Bray Ref Map Sheet 51 c F.14.b.5.5.	24/09/1918	26/09/1918
War Diary	Bray	26/09/1918	30/09/1918

Heading	War Diary 49 Divisional Trench Mortar Batteries for the month of October 1918. Vol 23.		
War Diary	Reference map Lens 11 1/100,000.		
War Diary	Brandt Camp	01/10/1918	09/10/1918
War Diary	Lens 2.I.2.1.3	09/10/1918	09/10/1918
War Diary	Cherisy Lens 4.K.9.2.77	09/10/1918	09/10/1918
War Diary	Reference Valenciennes. 1/100,000	10/10/1918	10/10/1918
War Diary	Billelts 4.c.60.12	10/10/1918	10/10/1918
War Diary	Escadoeuvres 4.D.25.25	12/10/1918	12/10/1918
War Diary	Naves	23/10/1918	23/10/1918
War Diary	4.D.42.78.	25/10/1918	25/10/1918
War Diary	Billets at 3.E.77.8.4.	28/10/1918	31/10/1918
War Diary	Reference map Valenciennes 1/100,000 Billelts at 3.E.77.8.4.		
War Diary	Bilelts at 3.E.77.8.4	01/11/1918	05/11/1918
War Diary	Bilelts at 2.G.31.12 Nr Valemciennes	06/11/1918	09/11/1918
War Diary	Erquennes 2.J.51.31	10/11/1918	27/11/1918
War Diary	Marly 2.G.5.2	28/11/1918	28/11/1918
War Diary	Mastaing 3.D.65.61	29/11/1918	30/11/1918
War Diary	Reference map Valenciennes 1/100,000		

WAR DIARY
or
INTELLIGENCE SUMMARY
(Erase heading not required.)

Army Form C. 2118

Instructions regarding War Diaries and Intelligence Summaries are contained in F. S. Regs., Part II. and the Staff Manual respectively. Title Pages will be prepared in manuscript.

Place	Date	Hour	Summary of Events and Information	Remarks and references to Appendices
	21.9.15	5.0AM	Bombardment still continues, whilst shrapnel were in action at time 9 rounds at enemy rifle from Nos 1 & 2 positions with successful effect. 3 Lancers (numbers) on & which got rifle aid.	
	22.9.15	"	Bombardment continued with more violence. Although our parapets were blown down all along the line & our communication with Gun positions were destroyed, it being impossible to recognise the trenches, it was found possible to rise along without cover & under heavy shell fire & to work the guns effectively. Nos 2 & 4 Guns front 5 rounds (high bursts), No 3 & 5 gun 16 rounds (shrapnel) throughout the day. No 3 Gun was not in action, however as it was not practice to fire on account of emplacement being again heavily damaged. It was very difficult to clearly observe the effect, on account of enemy position being jealously well hid, but on later observation it was certain that no enemy was sighted near our targets. Fairly quiet throughout the night.	
	23.9.15		Heavy Artillery firing continues. Considerable damage to our trenches, communication	

> # WAR DIARY
> ## or
> ## INTELLIGENCE SUMMARY
> *(Erase heading not required.)*

Army Form C. 2118

Instructions regarding War Diaries and Intelligence Summaries are contained in F.S. Regs., Part II. and the Staff Manual respectively. Title Pages will be prepared in manuscript.

Place	Date	Hour	Summary of Events and Information	Remarks and references to Appendices
	24.9.15	8.0 pm	Much machine gun firing in all about 30 bursts. One effect in enveloping wire of considerable importance. The firing throughout the day continuous. No 3 gun having been able only to fire light bursts on account of range, it was decided to alter the emplacement & to lower the gun on to a suitable target. This was completed late in the evening and no reports were taken. Capt. Firth takes over command.	
	25.9.15	4.0 am	Capt. Firth announces during hostilities L.W. Lawrence Lt. The information available I have hostilities was during attack.	
		5.0 pm	Have information that Capt Firth wounded & 2 missing. Go up to trench & take over command. I arrive about 7.30 after reporting to O.C. find the gun taken out to action men return to billets. Report to Staff Capt. round	
	26.9.15	10 pm	Instructions take gun into action immediately. Take up new detachment receive instructions from G.O.C. fire at craters	

WAR DIARY or INTELLIGENCE SUMMARY

Army Form C. 2118

Place	Date	Hour	Summary of Events and Information	Remarks and references to Appendices
	26.4.15	7.0pm	forward by name. On arrival at trenches report to C.O. to open communication with J.O.C. are wires not to be until own trestle are repaired. People are held up. Receive instructions from C.O. to take guns of 39th 39th batteries out of action. This wires cut to be answered by "Signals" a wire return. "Leave whenever to return" 39 39 trench howitzer batteries. This answer have read "Leave return etc" Report to S.O.C. ordered to return to again	
	27.4.15	7.0pm	Again requested by C.O. not to hire. Report to S.O.C and are then ordered to hire at crate. 39th 39th batteries are continued to take over commands of both.	
		5am	Repairs from 39th battery Higgins relieve me, trie from 39th 39th throughout the night.	
	28.4.15	9pm	Rgt. Surgn. Higgins relieves me, trie from 39th 39th howitzers at intervals throughout the day & night.	

WAR DIARY
or
INTELLIGENCE SUMMARY
(Erase heading not required.)

Army Form C. 2118

Place	Date	Hour	Summary of Events and Information	Remarks and references to Appendices
	28.9.15	7 am	Firing continued throughout the day at intervals with considerable effect. It being noticed on several occasions that fumes were made to belt from their position in the crater, once or twice torso, apparently arms, were blown into the air. Lt Trainer relieves Sgt Major Skippers	
	28.9.15	8 pm	I take over from Sgt Major Higgins. The C.O. regrets me not to fire during the night as the Battalion goes out tonight.	
	29.9.15	7 am	Firing is carried on throughout the day at intervals with good effect. Some rounds in the morning failed to explode but those in the afternoon a heavy bomb was fired into the crater and evidently set the other bombs, as three distinct explosions were observed.	
		7 pm	No firing was done during the night as the Infantry wanted to	

Army Form C. 2118

WAR DIARY
or
INTELLIGENCE SUMMARY
(Erase heading not required.)

Place	Date	Hour	Summary of Events and Information	Remarks and references to Appendices
	30.9.15	7am	Just on with the work of repairing their barbed wire. Firing continued at intervals during the day. Good effect was observed and all the shells exploded. The enemy retaliated with Trench Mortars and long bangs.	
		6pm	No firing was done at night as it was raining heavily and the C.O. thought it unnecessary to fire.	
	1.10.15	4 A.M.	Some good work was done in the morning. A heavy bomb was lured into the Crater and exploded. Immediately after a light bomb was fired into the German side of the crater when another body went up.	
		7.30pm	No firing took place at night.	
	2.10.15	7 A.M.	On firing in the morning. The enemy sent over some heavy bombs quite close to the gun emplacement. They were evidently searching for the gun. I therefore moved the gun to another emplacement and fired from that position.	
		8pm	Am relieved by Sgt Major Hood.	

No further to survey 2/Lt.

No further Harvey

Army Form C. 2118

WAR DIARY
or
INTELLIGENCE SUMMARY
(Erase heading not required.)

Instructions regarding War Diaries and Intelligence Summaries are contained in F.S. Regs., Part II. and the Staff Manual respectively. Title Pages will be prepared in manuscript.

Place	Date	Hour	Summary of Events and Information	Remarks and references to Appendices
	2.10.15	8 pm	Sgt Wood relieves 2 Lt Hurrey - reports to O.C. Infantry. Receive news that b/fire aiming apparatus, on account of working parties.	
	3.10.15	—	Receive orders to fire at intervals, particular attention being paid to the crater. 7 Rounds were fired midnight effect. No firing during daylight, at intervals.	
	4.10.15	—	12 Rounds fired, at intervals. 7 Rounds were effective 5 were blind. No firing during night.	
	5.10.15	—	13 Rounds fired sweeping the crater, 12 effective 3 blinds. No night firing.	
	6.10.15	—	11 Rounds fired, all effective and to target on the crater. We were not allowed to fire from 3 positions owing to our trench being badly battered during bombardment with many heavy howitzer & the Infantry working all in support. Returning orange two relievable was issued.	
		7.30	2 n/o L Cameron relieves.	

T. L. Cameron 2/Lt

WAR DIARY
or
INTELLIGENCE SUMMARY
(Erase heading not required.)

Army Form C. 2118

Instructions regarding War Diaries and Intelligence Summaries are contained in F. S. Regs., Part II. and the Staff Manual respectively. Title Pages will be prepared in manuscript.

Place	Date	Hour	Summary of Events and Information	Remarks and references to Appendices
	6.10.15	7-30	Relieve Sgt Flood. No firing at night.	
	7.10.15	4-30 am	Fire 3 rounds into crater with object of preventing proper keying up position in crater. This proves to be very effective & no firing was done from the position during the day. However firing at intervals, principally at the crater to destroy any work that may be done at night. No repair firing.	
	8.10.15	4-20 am	Repeat yesterday's firing at sappers position as effect. Industry report up to time at position where new work has been carried out & after registration this was bombed (apparently), the work apparently destroyed. Fire also during the day at intervals at crater. No night firing. 2nd Lt Taylor who joined battery on the 4th came to trenches + stays during relief.	
	9.10.15	4-30	Early firing continued. Need not to fire from	

WAR DIARY
or
INTELLIGENCE SUMMARY

Army Form C. 2118

Place	Date	Hour	Summary of Events and Information	Remarks and references to Appendices
	9/10/15		Spasmodic on account of, no damage however. I have to report a big percentage of "duds" during these days firing.	
	10.10.15		No fire at craters early in a.m. - harassing days & counter firing threat at intervals also at rest work done in enemy trenches & at various known snipers post. The firing generally was very effective. The Infantry h.o. acknowledge the good work done by Trench howitzers during these days.	M

JW Lawrence JLt.

Army Form C. 2118

WAR DIARY
or
INTELLIGENCE SUMMARY
(Erase heading not required.)

29.E39 Trench Mortar Btys

Instructions regarding War Diaries and Intelligence Summaries are contained in F.S. Regs., Part II. and the Staff Manual respectively. Title Pages will be prepared in manuscript.

Place	Date	Hour	Summary of Events and Information	Remarks and references to Appendices
	14-10-15		I relieved 2/Lieuts Harvey & Hutchison at 5 p.m. 14-10-15. They reported that both guns in A.1. trench had been taken out of action, their positions having been discovered & bombarded by hostile trench mortars. We received orders from Lt. Col: West to fire only in reply to enemy's trench mortars & not to fire during the night.	
	15-10-15		Received orders in the morning to open fire in conjunction with bombardment by our artillery which was to take place between 1 p.m. & 2 p.m. This bombardment was cancelled, but we fired three rounds in the afternoon into the crater (Point O4) one of them causing a second explosion. In the morning we removed the two gun beds in A.1. preparatory to setting up new positions for these guns.	
	16-10-15		This morning we fired three rounds into the crater from number 2 & 3 guns in H.18 & H.19. Mother received orders to dislodge a sniper who had been discovered in a position a few yards north of the crater. We fired three rounds each from No 2 & 3 guns – the two guns being fired simultaneously. The registration was good & the device could not be obtained so far as could be discovered. A few rounds were also fired into the crater.	
	17-10-15		About 5 a.m. this morning the enemy exploded a mine between his crater & H.20. An hour later, when hand bombs were being freely exchanged between the two craters, we fired a heavy bomb into the enemy's crater & apparently caused the enemy's bombing party to retire. We fired 2 more rounds & then received orders to fire into the crater every half hour of ¾ hour. This was done until midday when a further supply of 50 heavy bombs was received. We continued firing all day & throughout the night until midday on today morning.	
	18-10-15		This morning a new position for one of the guns from A.1. was taken up to command the crater & duly registered. After midday we received orders to slacken fire & and occasional shots into the crater. I was relieved at 4.30 p.m. by 2/Lieut. Hutchison.	

C.C.O. Taylor
2/Lieut. 3/10ᵗʰ R⁵ Trench Mortar Batty.
20 – 10 – 15.

1875 Wt. W593/826 1,000,000 4/15 J.B.C. & A. A.D.S.S./Forms/C. 2118.

Army Form C. 2118

WAR DIARY
—or—
INTELLIGENCE SUMMARY
(Erase heading not required.)

29 Z 39 Trench Mortar Bys.

Place	Date	Hour	Summary of Events and Information	Remarks and references to Appendices
	18.10.15.		I relieved 2/Lieut Taylor at 4.30 pm 18.10.15. We received orders from Lt. Col. Webb to fire occasional rounds into the trenches (Point 04) during the night which proved effective, and we received wild retaliation.	
	19.10.15.		We received orders in the morning to fire occasional rounds into the trenches. Offset mid-day the enemy had over several bombs from a gun which the division we located and replied with several trench mortars with effect; Enemy didn't reply. During the night we fired several rounds at irregular intervals into the trenches.	
	20.10.15.		We received orders to fire into enemy communication trench leading into trenches. The registration was good as a portion of the trench was blown in. The enemy then replied from a position very left, but all bombs fell short. We located their gun, the range being too great. I reported same to Artillery Officer who dealt with them successfully. During the night we fired several rounds into the trenches.	
	21.10.15.		We received orders to fire into communication trench, also trench at intervals the fire being effective, and blowing up enemy's trench more. No firing during night.	
	22.10.15.		Orders were then received to fire only in reply to enemy trench mortars, when several light bombs from the 3 gun were fired into communication trench. I was relieved at 2 pm by 2/Lieut J. Longbourne R.G.A. 26th Trench Mortar Battery 4th Division Battery being ordered out for rest.	

Alexander Auchinon
2/Lieut. Staff Off. Trench Mortar Batt
3rd Divisional Artillery 24.10.15

WAR DIARY
or
INTELLIGENCE SUMMARY

Army Form C. 2118

Place	Date	Hour	Summary of Events and Information	Remarks and references to Appendices
Trenches	22.10.15 to 31.10.15		29th – 39th Battns, 14th Division, out of action + resting at farm G 4 c 6 3 Sheet 28.	

Army Form C. 2118

29 & 39 *French Weather Extract*

WAR DIARY
or
INTELLIGENCE SUMMARY
(Erase heading not required.)

Place	Date	Hour	Summary of Events and Information	Remarks and references to Appendices
Riulé	31-10-15 to 6/11/15		29th & 39th Battns. at rest in Riulé. G.4.c.6.3. Sheet 28. Men engaged breeding wooden huts etc. for winter accommodation, & in drainage. Some day all ranks are given we have bayonet drill & two classes in telephony are continued under qualified N.C.O's. Training and of action are daily carried out also. Tho Lawrence Lt. a/Lt 2nd Bn Rs— OC 29 & 39 2nd Bn Rs—	

Place	Date	Hour	Summary of Events and Information	Remarks and references to Appendices
POPERINGHE	7.11.15		29th - 7/39th Trench Mortar Batteries at rest at G.38.10.1 Sheet 28 Men occupies building huts accommodation, continue classes in signalling & telephony. Every day physical drill is taken for men keen & the men are also instructed in the use of smoke helmets & N.C.O's practices in firing men without removing the helmet. 3 N.C.O's then sent to 14 & 6th Div. Bomb. School for instruction. 2nd Lieut (R.O.) Taylor transfers to 6th Div: & goes into action with 38th Battery	

WAR DIARY
or
INTELLIGENCE SUMMARY
(Erase heading not required.)

Army Form C. 2118

29² 39 [illegible] Motor [illegible]

Place	Date	Hour	Summary of Events and Information	Remarks and references to Appendices
	7.11.15		Have note that recommendation of 2/Lt KNIVETON for commission No 53850, R.G.A., is approved & this officer left for England to rejt.	
	8.11.15 to 10		Continue typical transpt, lorrophor, leesphong & bicciwp [?] training.	
	11.11.15			
	12.11.15		2nd Lieut Inglis returns from duty with 6th Bn.	
	13.11.15		Continue with daily routine as above.	

[signature] J W Jameson ?
at In. [illegible] suppi.

K 15/11

WAR DIARY
or
INTELLIGENCE SUMMARY

(Erase heading not required.)

Army Form C. 2118

Instructions regarding War Diaries and Intelligence Summaries are contained in F.S. Regs., Part II. and the Staff Manual respectively. Title Pages will be prepared in manuscript.

Place	Date	Hour	Summary of Events and Information	Remarks and references to Appendices
Spanybr	14/11/15		Battene 29/39 Trenes Monitzys scale at rest at G4 c 6 3. Sheet 28. Parrots continued as usual. 1e Physical drill, bayonet, telephony, lectures however in use of Lewis Kennets.	
	15/11/15		Kit Inspection. Parrots as above	
	16/11/15		Parrots as 14.11.15	
	17/11/15		" 15.11.15	
	18/11/15		Parrots as usual. 2nd Lieuts D. Frant & E.E. Cole joined from Divisional batteries, are posted to 29th & 39th Trench Mortar Brigade, & are respectively becomes responsing.	

Army Form C. 2118

WAR DIARY
or
INTELLIGENCE SUMMARY
(Erase heading not required.)

Instructions regarding War Diaries and Intelligence Summaries are contained in F. S. Regs., Part II. and the Staff Manual respectively. Title Pages will be prepared in manuscript.

Place	Date	Hour	Summary of Events and Information	Remarks and references to Appendices
	19-11-15		All Officers & men of 39 & 64 Battery start in one trip convoy to transfer at 10 & Divisionaire Brigade School. 2nd Lieut Harvey reports from Hospital to duty.	
	20-11-15		Is in action & takes over position of A.6. proceeding heretofore by 38 Battery of 6th Div. Also relieve the 14th Battery 6th Div. but as they had not newly been in action to 6th Div area, no records were left to place any guns — that particular sector battle instructions received from headquarters 1st Division. RFA relieving position of 38 Battery battery division to have been over 3 1/2 hours.	RA 24/11

1875 Wt. W593/826 1,000,000 4/15 J.B.C. & A. A.D.S.S./Forms/C. 2118.

Army Form C. 2118

29 & 39 Trench Mortar Batteries

WAR DIARY
or
INTELLIGENCE SUMMARY
(Erase heading not required.)

Instructions regarding War Diaries and Intelligence Summaries are contained in F. S. Regs., Part II. and the Staff Manual respectively. Title Pages will be prepared in manuscript.

Place	Date	Hour	Summary of Events and Information	Remarks and references to Appendices
	30.11.15 onds		2 Lt Hutchinson in command, 1 & 2nd Lieut Jones for Instruction proceed, one N.C.O + men, Nuch - Return of 2 NCO's & 8 men at a present time to HQ YPRES @ I7A59	
	31.11.15		& receipt telg place and permanent biller Headquarters. Am a fatigue unpaid to refer from Infantry Division Commander had 2 Lt killed continue issue forwards as Stypical snow, by winning etc.	Dep'n

J W Jameson Lt
Lt Col i/c 2 W Battn
O.C. 1st & Div 2 M. Battalion

1875 Wt. W593/826 1,000,000 4/15 J.B.C. & A. A.D.S.S./Forms/C. 2118.

WAR DIARY
INTELLIGENCE SUMMARY
(Erase heading not required.)

Army Form C. 2118

Place	Date	Hour	Summary of Events and Information	Remarks and references to Appendices
	22.11.15		Orders were received to fire in retaliation only; no rounds were fired. The position being quiet. The day was spent in cleaning gun position. Also repairing dug-outs which we found to be in a very bad state.	
	23.11.15		We were busy repairing wood-stand, building a new floor with sandbags. Dug-outs were also improved. The position being quiet - no rounds were fired.	
	24.11.15		Not considering gun positions sufficient we started building a new emplacement with which foundation at CRUMP FARM in A.6. I was relieved at 4 pm. 24.11.15 by 2/Lt. Taylor. Infantry was down during this day.	

Alexander Hutchison
2/Lt.
29th Trench Mortar Battery

Army Form C. 2118

29 & 39th Trench Mortar Batty

WAR DIARY

INTELLIGENCE SUMMARY

(Erase heading not required.)

Instructions regarding War Diaries and Intelligence Summaries are contained in F. S. Regs., Part II. and the Staff Manual respectively. Title Pages will be prepared in manuscript.

Place	Date	Hour	Summary of Events and Information	Remarks and references to Appendices
	24-11-15		2/Lieut: E.G. Porter & myself relieved 2/Lieuts: Hutchison & Grant about 7 p.m. We did no night firing.	AJ/15
	25-11-15		This day was spent in preparing a new emplacement at CRUMP FARM to command the MOUND & enfilade the app to the MOUND. The Colonel of the 7th R.B. suggested that we should examine a suspected sniper's post near ODER HOUSES which we did about midnight but apparently it was unoccupied. No rounds fired.	
	26-11-15		The new position was continued to be prepared & the guns (N° 2 & 3) left by the 6th Division were registered. The former registers were found to be incorrect. The Colonel suggested an emplacement in A.8. to command the german point 80.	
	27-11-15		This morning we went to A.8. & found it to be practically unapproachable owing to water & we could find no suitable position. The new emplacement (N°1) was finished this day. No rounds were fired.	
	28-11-15		We obtained good registers this day with N°s 1 & 2 guns - the latter falling in very close proximity to a fire, the smoke of which was very noticeable. 2/Lieut: Hutchison relieved us about 7 p.m.	

C.C.O. Taylor
2/Lieut.
39th T.M. Batty.

29 Trench Mortar Battery

WAR DIARY
INTELLIGENCE SUMMARY
(Erase heading not required.)

Army Form C. 2118

Place	Date	Hour	Summary of Events and Information	Remarks and references to Appendices
	28.11.15		I relieved 2/Lt. Taylor at 7pm. 28.11.15. Orders were received to fire during night in retaliation. The position being quiet no rounds were fired.	
	29.11.15		At day-break two rounds were fired from gun 2.5.3. the registration being good, but both rounds were ineffective. I received orders that a new position should be taken up in A.8 trench, but owing to the flooded state of the trenches it was found impossible to obtain same. During the afternoon I altered several fuses, then fired two rounds from No.1 gun, the target being green mound, the registration was good, and the second bomb most effective, being a large crater. I received orders from the Colonel to fire in retaliation only during the night. no rounds were fired.	
	30.11.15		Two rounds were fired from No.1 gun at day-break the target being the green mound, one round effective. The enemy retaliation by snipers and several whiz bangs, which shifted the gun bed, but no damage was done. We worked remainder of day draining, and repairing gun position in A.C. trench. Been relieved by 2/Lt. Taylor at 7.pm. 30.11.15.	

Alexander Hutcheson 2/Lt
29 Trench Mortar Battery

~~2 ARMY~~

49 DIV

34

TRENCH MORTAR
BTY

1915 JULY TO 1915 DEC

WAR DIARY
or
INTELLIGENCE SUMMARY
(Erase heading not required.)

Army Form C. 2118

Place	Date	Hour	Summary of Events and Information	Remarks and references to Appendices
	9/7/15	10 pm	Battery arrived BERTHEN.	
	10/7/15	9 pm	Took out gun at 3.30 pm. Bombs 12.18 pm bombs withe whole battery and mounted gun 30 behind fire trench in enflicement its fire and good difficulty in getting but slay anyway tried.	
	11/7/15	9 am	Kept Mpt. shot on man with gun from 10.30 pm bombs at salient Range 160. Kept no reply. Burst damage to parapet. 1st round got 2 out but registered. after 5 rounds no German reply and had shifts a lot at registration.	
	12/7/15	4 am	Fired 11.30 pm bombs at 5 am Salient as German had been annoying before in working parties the night before. Same range. Two shells on Burg would. Sent would not go into bomb.	
	13/7/15	10 a.m	Reconnoitred position for another gun opposite another salient. got up remains of arm from DA to Reels. Bombardment with gun shells in enough of which wreck gun emplacement but no damage done.	
	14/7/15	9 pm	Remounted gun in new position.	
	15/7/15	9 pm	Tried to get up second gun but railway had been damaged in last the next night.	

Army Form C. 2118

WAR DIARY
or
INTELLIGENCE SUMMARY
(Erase heading not required.)

Instructions regarding War Diaries and Intelligence Summaries are contained in F. S. Regs., Part II. and the Staff Manual respectively. Title Pages will be prepared in manuscript.

Place	Date	Hour	Summary of Events and Information	Remarks and references to Appendices
	16.7.15	2 p.m	Got up 2nd gun and 10 rds 2.3 p.m and 6.15 p.m. Right trav. unit to dig emplacement, as ground is too wet.	
	17.7.15	10 a.m	Dug emplacement off communication trench 20 yds in rear of parapet.	
	18.7.15	5 p.m	Reconnoitre position for gun on left of the line. Find best method of carrying load is to carry it upside down on the porter bars. With two stretcher slings round the man's neck. The load does not then get in the way of their legs and they can carry it a long way without fatigue. I recommend the issue of a pair of stretcher slings with each gun.	

STRETCHER
SLINGS

BED

Nitzwalah Capt R.H.A.
Cmdg 34 T.H. Batten.

Army Form C. 2118

WAR DIARY
or
INTELLIGENCE SUMMARY
(Erase heading not required.)

Instructions regarding War Diaries and Intelligence Summaries are contained in F.S. Regs., Part II. and the Staff Manual respectively. Title Pages will be prepared in manuscript.

Place	Date	Hour	Summary of Events and Information	Remarks and references to Appendices
+D+7	18.7.15		Reconnoitred position for Howitzer on left of 14.B Bdes against a new trench the germans are making.	
	19.7.15		Visited french trenches to find position for Howitzer but found the new trench was in dead ground. Back Howitzer quiet except for eight bombs or grenades thrown in the morning as the germans have been	
	20.7.15		Arranged to fire with No.1 gun with bombards with Howitzer	
	21.7.15	a.m.	Germans lay quieter down so did not fire.	
		3 p.m	to Whitefer arrived.	
		9 p.m	got up gun and with party on left of 14.B Bdes and dug position for gun 30× in rear of fire trench. Ground very wet and came trench alongside gun emplacement.	
	22.7.15	9 a.m	Arranged for drainage of new gun position which was very wet after the rain.	
		1 p.m	Fired ten rounds from No. 2 gun. two blinds. Shew in a fair command of parapet, mortar, bombs and grenades returned but gun emplacement was not hit. Range 65 yds.	
		5 p.m	To Dick joins the division	
	23.7.15	10 a.m	Reconnoitred position for two howitzers on right of 14.7 Bde. against two bombs which an been built.	

N.R. Walch Capt. R.H.A.
Cmdg 36 T.H. Battr.

25/7/15

Army Form C. 2118

34 T French How By

WAR DIARY
or
INTELLIGENCE SUMMARY
(Erase heading not required.)

Instructions regarding War Diaries and Intelligence Summaries are contained in F.S. Regs., Part II. and the Staff Manual respectively. Title Pages will be prepared in manuscript.

Place	Date	Hour	Summary of Events and Information	Remarks and references to Appendices
	25.7.15	4 a.m.	Quiet day all along the line. Visit all guns of 148 Bde.	
	26.7.15	2 p.m.	Sent to Whitehu to BERTHEN to bring up 42nd T.H. Battery. Visit 147 Bde guns.	
	27.7.15	3 a.m.	7 in gun rounds from left of line in reply to bombs, which quiets matters down.	
			Reconnoitre and make a sketch of left had trenches.	
	28.7.15	11 a.m.	Pony Battery. Artillery bombardment in afternoon against top head opposite to 42nd Bty, arriving with Whitaker and Kennedy.	
			2 gun. Visit all the guns. no firing. 42nd Bty arrives with Whitaker and Kennedy.	
	29.7.15	10 a.m.	Take Kennedy up to right Brigade trenches and reconnoitre positions for their guns there which he gets in position at night.	
			Reallot Batteries as follows.	
			34 Battery 148 Bde Left.	
			37 Battery 147 Bde Centre.	
			42 Battery 146 Bde Right.	
	30.7.15	2 p.m.	Reconnoitre position for a third gun of 34 Bty on left of line.	
		4 p.m.	Take up gun and get it into position. While so doing violent bombing began against advanced trench. Fire ten rounds from other gun which quiets matters at once. Twelve rounds fired at gun which all fall 100ft over.	
	31.7.15	2 p.m.	Visit 137 Bty and have ten rounds at redoubt, one below. Germans again reply but their rounds fall well over.	Nitrehold Capt R.14 A

1/8/15

J? 2/8/15

WAR DIARY
or
INTELLIGENCE SUMMARY   34. T.M. Battery.

XLIX   Army Form C. 2118

Place	Date	Hour	Summary of Events and Information	Remarks and references to Appendices
C.7.c.2.8.	8.8.	6.30 p.m	Bombard enemy wire with eight guns. (4.34″ + 2.37″ + 2.42″) 150 light bombs had been issued and only 25 heavy were available. No report of attack. One man wounded.	
		9 p.m	Withdrew six guns and attachments leaving all the bombs.	
	9.8.		Quiet day, nothing doing.	
	10.8.	3 a.m	Fired 7 light and 5 heavy bombs in reply to heavy bombardment enemy's trench mortars. Two hits on parapet. Observation difficult owing to mist. Silenced the enemy mortars.	
	11.8.	3 p.m	Fired two light bombs in reply to enemy mortars and to develop own.	
		8 p.m	Violent hand bombs thrown by enemy against advanced trench. Fired two heavy bombs into his bank which caused him to desist at once.	
	12.8.	7 a.m	Violent bombardment by 3 enemy mortars. Fired 7 heavy and 1 light in reply which failed to silence him. Had to stop from lack of heavy bombs. Several rounds effective in trench then tried to get a hit on enemy's emplacement without success.	

JK 20/9/15

WAR DIARY
or
INTELLIGENCE SUMMARY
(Erase heading not required.)

Army Form C. 2118

34 ⁊⁊⁊⁊ 34/7/41/67

Place	Date	Hour	Summary of Events and Information	Remarks and references to Appendices
	12.8.	4.30 p.m	Violent bombardment by four enemy mortars mostly "Minnenjars". Was unable to reply as no heavy bombs remained and light bombs ineffective at this range. The P.O. had burned 4 officers of Minnenjar.	
	13.8.	5 p	Another violent "Minnenjar" bombardment replied and one light bombers two of which burst the enemy trench. Several silenced, him for the moment.	
	14.8.	3 p.m	Very heavy bombardment by this Minnenjar mortars, one of which blew in the gun dug out killing Bt= Ryan and bunging the same of the detachment. Replied with eight light bombs, of which two bars aided to get the upper hand own in the trench, blowing up the contents. Failed in the trenches, blowing up the contents. Failed to [illegible] equipoise in weight of enemy ordnance.	
		9 p.m	With remission of Brig. Genl. 148" Brigade the two guns were withdrawn from this position, as they further had been accurately located by enemy mortars, and we were unable to reply effectively with light bombs the only ammunition available. Reconnoitred another position further to the right.	

Netheidal Capt R.H.A.
Comdg 34th = T.H. Butler

16/8/15.

WAR DIARY
or
INTELLIGENCE SUMMARY
(Erase heading not required.)

Army Form C. 2118

34th Batty
34
Position of Battr. B.29.a.

Place	Date	Hour	Summary of Events and Information	Remarks and references to Appendices
	16.8		Reconnoitred new position for guns. Got up wire leads and one gun at night and dug them in.	
	17.8		Cleared remaining leads and ammunition from old position and continued digging new position.	
	18.8		Our new emplacement blown in. Finished dug outs and other gun position. Gun damaged.	
	19.8		Quiet day. Le Epine paper battery.	
	20.8		Building dug outs.	
	21.8		Quiet day. Made new emplacement at night. Finished emplacement and deepened dug outs.	
	22.8		Quiet day on the left this week. Infantry remained to our line on the enemy were quiet, and only light bombs start bang as the enemy were quiet, and only light bombs available.	24/8/15

Major Cmdg 34. T.H. Batty

Cmdg 34. T.H. Batty

34ᵗʰ T.H. Battery.

Army Form C. 2118

WAR DIARY
or
INTELLIGENCE SUMMARY

34 T.H. [illegible signature]

(Erase heading not required.)

Instructions regarding War Diaries and Intelligence Summaries are contained in F.S. Regs., Part II. and the Staff Manual respectively. Title Pages will be prepared in manuscript.

Place	Date	Hour	Summary of Events and Information	Remarks and references to Appendices
22.8.15.				
	23.8		Capt Tuck W.R. Regt joined the observers.	
	24.8		Infantry from 14ᵗʰ Bde arrived. 2 N.C.O's and 10 men. Put new lead from H Army wirehead into position with 37ᵗʰ Bty.	
	25.8	4 am	Fired 2 heavy and 7 light bombs in reply to enemy "Rum Jars". The enemy was too weak to see the result. Reconnaissance near position unfortunately but work of use unfinished.	
		6 pm	Taken near lead wire to light bombs very unsuccessful.	
	26.8.		Quiet day.	
	27.8	4 pm	Fired two bomb bombs in reply to enemy mortars. Result damage to property doubt and articles presumably for dustless.	
	28.8		Capt Tuck joins 14ᵗʰ Division	

30/8/15

Attended Capt R.H.A
Comdg 34 T.H. Bty.

[signature] 1/9/15

WAR DIARY 34th T.H Battery, Army Form C. 2118
or
INTELLIGENCE SUMMARY

Place	Date	Hour	Summary of Events and Information	Remarks and references to Appendices
	30th August to 4 September		No firing was done the whole of the week, as new enemy's trench mortars fired along this front. Week occupied in improving trenches and reliveting after the heavy rains of the last three days.	

6/9/15

Wilson Colt. Capt. R.H.A.
Comdg 34. T.H. Batty. 4th A. Div.

9/9/15

Army Form C. 2118

WAR DIARY
or
INTELLIGENCE SUMMARY
(Erase heading not required.)

34th Tunnel Howitzer Battery

Instructions regarding War Diaries and Intelligence Summaries are contained in F.S. Regs., Part II. and the Staff Manual respectively. Title Pages will be prepared in manuscript.

Place	Date	Hour	Summary of Events and Information	Remarks and references to Appendices
In the field	12.9.15		Position in Wyatt Lane occupied, found 12 thousand rounds in Fortin 17 starting a fire on the ammunition store which burned for 10 minutes, illuminated shed. Enemy heavy informed enemy during night	
	13.9.15		Completed dug out and land telephone wires. Gave you fire on Wyatt Lane behind F.31. Fired 6 rounds at Fortin 14 on establishing all telescoped posts. Enemy day and one night burst. Four fused day out one others left. Repeatedly telephoned wires.	
	14.9.15		Observed trenches, looks very quiet, probably the result of previous sharp	
	15.9.15		Dropping manoeuvring at Basel	
	16.9.15		Quiet on enemy's, our left infantry infantry attacked large works (two bound) but could not allow us to fire	
	17.9.15			
	18.9.15		Enemy maintained an extreme left upon our front. line never exploding shell cases little, shape being defective	

W. Dennes Hand R. F. O.
34 Tunnel How. Battery

Army Form C. 2118

WAR DIARY
or
INTELLIGENCE SUMMARY 34th of Trench Mow Bay

(Erase heading not required.)

Instructions regarding War Diaries and Intelligence Summaries are contained in F. S. Regs., Part II. and the Staff Manual respectively. Title Pages will be prepared in manuscript.

Place	Date	Hour	Summary of Events and Information	Remarks and references to Appendices
Spitalfield	19/9/15		Shepherded trench to center gun improving same.	
	20/9/15		Built dug out for right gun	
	21/9/15		Tested telephone wires & needed same	
	22/9/15		Strengthened walls of dug-out on right gun & started work on a bomb store	
	23/9/15		Built bomb store for centre gun	
	24/9/15		Improving trench & round parapet leading to right gun, left gun first six rounds	
	25/9/15		Artillery bombarding. Right trenches left gun fired six rounds (Two men's duty)	
			All bombs got well into Boche trenches. Two close to their parties, which did not fire again. Being bombarded by artillery one of our gunners carried a Boche into trench to the obstruction of the great annoyance of the own infantry.	

A.S. Stevens Capt
O/C T.M. Bay
28/9/15

Army Form C. 2118

34 Trench Mortar Battery

WAR DIARY
or
INTELLIGENCE SUMMARY
(Erase heading not required.)

Instructions regarding War Diaries and Intelligence Summaries are contained in F. S. Regs., Part II. and the Staff Manual respectively. Title Pages will be prepared in manuscript.

Place	Date	Hour	Summary of Events and Information	Remarks and references to Appendices
In the field	26/9/15		Quiet. Laying trench grids.	
	27/9/15		Quiet. Heavy rain.	
	28/9/15		Draining trenches between showers. No 1 Gun flooded, raised bed to prevent same damming position.	
	29/9/15		Cleaning trenches round guns.	
	30/9/15		No 1 gun nearly collapsed, commenced bomb store on right gun.	
	1/10/15		Completed bomb store. Commenced clearing trench for front line. Had No 2 Gun to support trench.	
	2/10/15		Note. Last week, only a small bomb or two being thrown into our trenches doing no damage. Trenches in a flooded condition round our positions which I am improving so that no trouble.	

7/10/15

N Devonald
OC 34 T.M.B.

Army Form C. 2118

WAR DIARY
or
INTELLIGENCE SUMMARY
(Erase heading not required.)

34 T.M. Battery

Place	Date	Hour	Summary of Events and Information	Remarks and references to Appendices
Littlefield	3/9/15		Continued clearing trenches and further Projected No 2 Bomb store from wet. Quiet.	
	4/9/15		Deepening and clearing trench No 2 gun. Quiet.	
	5/9/15		Lengthened & improved dug out on right gun. Quiet.	
	6/9/15		Laying trench grids. Quiet.	
	7/9/15		Continued Afinished grinding trench from fire trench front No 2 gun to outpost trench. Quiet.	
	8/9/15		Commenced clearing disused infantry support trench, having Officers dug out on way to No 2 gun. Quiet.	
	9/9/15		Continued above. Quiet	

M Donvala 2/LRFA
O/C 34 T.M.B.

Army Form C. 2118

WAR DIARY
or
INTELLIGENCE SUMMARY
(Erase heading not required.)

34 Trench Mortar Batt

Place	Date	Hour	Summary of Events and Information	Remarks and references to Appendices
Battlefield	10/10/15 11/10/15		Working on back trench, rebuilt parapet at top of communication trench (water gag) Repairing trenches and relaying telephone wires from No1 to No2 gun 2-3 p.m. enemy mortar fire Total 7 opened fire. Finding of the gun and several unreliable bombs, we returned promptly with No1 gun, meaning the enemy fire, we fired between our sights. 5 lights were duds and one premature. To any out who reported them up.	
	12/10/15 13/10/15		Quiet day, continued deepening trenches. Carried out demonstration with divisional artillery. My offgun, F23 fired at intervals of 5 minutes sweeping from line 8 trees to canal track. All detonated and we had little reply. No1 Mor gun and fired in conjunction. Meaning near No3 gun & controlling fire by telephone fired 3 HE & 20 light 85mm intervals together with No2 heavies into Trench 7 & light sweeping turret when inside gun heavy fired together Enemy replied with min gans and light bombs. Loss of wheel made bullets. I then searched for maintenance at forth detonation of trench 7, their aim for the cane gun, however at 3 my range Total fired were 10 Heavy & 30 light for the Cane guns, Henry two a cud and 1 premature at 190 yards and 8 lights were duds. Stan & faulty order. Effect- parapet damaged and quite a victim for our mortars.	
	14/10/15 15/10/15 16/10/15		Constructed another bomb store near No3 gun for reserve bombs. Quiet day. Removed same duds from old forward position at T33. to new position behind No3 gun. Heavy Boche demonstration to our right, we were quiet however. I reached on left infantry to right.	

R Donald Cpt/TCRA
OC 34 T.M.B.

No 2740

Army Form C. 2118

34th Trench Mortar Bty
49th Division

WAR DIARY
INTELLIGENCE SUMMARY
(Erase heading not required.)

Instructions regarding War Diaries and Intelligence Summaries are contained in F.S. Regs., Part II. and the Staff Manual respectively. Title Pages will be prepared in manuscript.

Place	Date	Hour	Summary of Events and Information	Remarks and references to Appendices
In the field	24th Oct		Quiet day, completed servant's dug-out.	
" "	25th "	"	Took over E.29 from 4.3 Battery (Temporarily) placed 2 beds in position one trained on German salient between E.29 & other on trenches to right. Hangan	
" "	26th "	"	Clearing trenches, which were very bad owing to the rain during the previous night. Quiet day.	
" "	27th "	"	Continued clearing Trenches. Tested Telephone wires. Enemy's artillery active behind our lines. (Quiet in the trenches)	
" "	28th "	"	Very heavy rain, just flooring bunker in Bomb. Store (No 2 gun) selected sites for reserve beds.	
" "	29th "	"	Put in new emplacement in second line, for No 3 gun to be able to enfilade our front line in case of attack. Quiet	
" "	30th "	"	Put in two 4 pounders, one on right & one on extreme left, clearing up trenches. Enemy Quiet.	

R.S. Jenning Lt. R.A. Regt
for O.C. 34 T. Bty

1875 Wt. W593/826 1,000,000 4/15 J.B.C. & A. A.D.S.S./Forms/C. 2118.

Army Form C. 2118.

WAR DIARY
or
INTELLIGENCE SUMMARY.

(Erase heading not required.)

34 Trench Mortar Battery

Place	Date	Hour	Summary of Events and Information	Remarks and references to Appendices
In the field	28/15		Billet. 20.000 Sh. 28.N.W B.19. b.8.5.	
	29/15		Fatigue party to old Bocat collecting R.E. material etc.	
	30/15		Building latrines etc.	
	1/2		Instruction on 1½" mortar.	
	2/15		Fatigue party to canal bank constructing dugout.	
	3/15		Fatigue party to canal bank carrying flooring material for dug out	
	4/15		Building incinerator	

J. C. Stees Capt.
19th (W.R.) W.O. T.M. Batt

N. D. ——— It 34 T.M.B.

WAR DIARY
or
INTELLIGENCE SUMMARY

Army Form C. 2118

(Erase heading not required.)

34 Trench Mortar Battery

Place	Date	Hour	Summary of Events and Information	Remarks and references to Appendices
296 field	21/5		Billet. 2000. Sht. 28. N.W. B.19. c.8.5.	
	22/5		Strengthening billets. Commenced dug out on canal bank. Continued strengthening billets.	
	23/5		Cleaning up 1½" ammunition.	
	24/5		Removed all stores to cellar in new billet. Everybody slept at new billet.	
	25/5		all men moved from billet at 5 pm. Everybody animals, mun[?] walked to tent site. Carried down 10 cwt stores for T.M. to ammunition store.	
	26/5			
	27/5		Clearing up old billets, animals etc and removing R.E. stores.	

M Desmond 2/Lt R.G.A.
O/c 34 T.M.B.

Army Form C. 2118

WAR DIARY
or
INTELLIGENCE SUMMARY
(Erase heading not required.)

34 Trench Mortar Battery

Place	Date	Hour	Summary of Events and Information	Remarks and references to Appendices
In the field F.31 - 35	14/11/15		Position of Battery. 20.000 sheet 28. N.W. B.2.Y. Central	
	15/11/15		Removed bed and telephone and storm from P.31 as trenches were blown & fallen in. Had attempts there first to remove two from dugouts two & no. 4 - Failed, bedding unless written & quite immovable.	
	16/11/15		Brought down there since 10 bombs from Hyatts Farm to Canal Bank. Stopped all night near 4 howitzer gun in Tangate.	
	17/11/15		Now very shorthanded gun in case of emergency. Quiet day.	
	18/11/15		Fatigue party to canal bank to bring down all type leads.	
	19/11/15		Clean up old ammunition & getting same in order.	
	20/11/15		Strengthening billets, sandbagging & attending roofs.	

N. Denner 2/Lt R.G.A.
O/C 34 T.M.B.

WAR DIARY or INTELLIGENCE SUMMARY

Army Form C. 2118

34 Trench Mortar Battery

Place	Date	Hour	Summary of Events and Information	Remarks and references to Appendices
2nd Life field F.31 - F.35.	7/11/15 8/11/15		Sheet 28NW B.2.q.3.3 - Rellt. Refixing gun position in F.33. Took out fuzes, telephone, charges, Tools etc from totem.)	
		About 5pm	Enemy sent out some rifle grenades at F.33, we retaliated with 4 rounds & 4 rounds with good effect.	
	9/11/15		Enemy position in Wyatt's lane.	
	10/11/15		Raced bed in position in forward trench F.35, primarily to search for enemies mortar opposite the trench. As I could not locate mortar exactly even from forward lines from where it appeared to far back for 1½" gun to reach, stick gun to enfilade German trench. Combt up 10 heavy rounds.	
	11/11/15	11 am.	Fired gun F 35, after 6 rounds enemy mortar opened fire on our Barry in French behind no. Completed the 10 rounds & reached position carrying out gun totoke. Eight detonated 5" clear in enemy trench & the others we felt into carnade out to our that morning. The enemy mortar (now fiv'd by 7(4) attempted us and it was impossible in my opinion to silence it until 1½ mortar). This gun in F.33, tried to silence fire on us firing 1 heavy & 1 4pdnr. This had tin of gum. We caused it return 4 mortar fine & fixed 1 rnd. The detonated in german trench. Every gun fired at present so little cover except enemy soft our gun at rest. Heavy rain, by this time position rapidly becoming untenable. Total 17, F31. Took out 1 bed and 10 tools from F.31.	Note 34 T.M.B.
	13/11/15		Gun unfavorable for mountings for weeks.	

No. 34 T.M.B.
OC. 34 T.M.B.

Army Form C. 2118

WAR DIARY
or
INTELLIGENCE SUMMARY

24 Trench Mortar Battery

(Erase heading not required.)

Instructions regarding War Diaries and Intelligence Summaries are contained in F.S. Regs., Part II. and the Staff Manual respectively. Title Pages will be prepared in manuscript.

Place	Date	Hour	Summary of Events and Information	Remarks and references to Appendices
Lole field	31/9/15		Rain, trenches filling in	
Bucy	1/10/15		Continuous rain, gun positions at F31+7 under water & untenable.	
S 7 & N.W. 2/10/15			Trench Mortar Bed carried up as it was possible and gun to be used if necessary, drawing positions	
A 33				
B & 9.	3/10/15		Mae rain and gun at F 31 removed	
Battery	4/10/15		drawing left position and cleared dug out.	
F 31 - 35.	5/10/15		Still flooded and trench has down to canal bank	
	6/10/15		same.	

K MM/15

6 November 21 R.G.A.
O.C. 24th Trench Mortar Battery.

Army Form C. 2118.

WAR DIARY
or
INTELLIGENCE SUMMARY.
(Erase heading not required.)

3 & 4 Trench Mortar Battery

Instructions regarding War Diaries and Intelligence Summaries are contained in F. S. Regs., Part II. and the Staff Manual respectively. Title pages will be prepared in manuscript.

Place	Date	Hour	Summary of Events and Information	Remarks and references to Appendices
S. of la Folie	11/9/15		Strengthened dug out & sand bank.	
	12/9/15		Completed above emplacement and were dug out.	
	14/9/15		Fatigue party carrying up gun stores.	
	15/9/15		Started second reserve emplacement to cover F.35 trench.	
	16/9/15			
	17/9/15		Fatigue party carrying to Cavalry & howitzer gun behind F.21 to support trench.	
	18/9/15		Moved 4 pdr & reserve trench to sec F.21. if required, also 4 pdr & 1½" gun to cover F.32-35. Did not find emplacement at R.E.A.	

M. Desvoeux Capt
O/C 3 & 4 T.M.B.

2L 28 NW B 19, & 25.

Army Form C. 2118.

WAR DIARY
or
INTELLIGENCE SUMMARY.
(Erase heading not required.)

Instructions regarding War Diaries and Intelligence Summaries are contained in F. S. Regs., Part II. and the Staff Manual respectively. Title pages will be prepared in manuscript.

Place	Date	Hour	Summary of Events and Information	Remarks and references to Appendices
	Friday 21/7/15	—	Day left Doelen. Carried rain all day. Finished tent improvements.	JHB
	Wed 22/7/15		Reconnaissance of the front. Selected emplacement for four guns. Two to E.3. & G.1. Two to E.2. & F.5. Moved R.V. from Cookham to B.R.S.C.	JHB
	Thursday 23/7/15		Prepared emplacements & ammunition dugout. Too hot to work.	JHB
	Friday 24/7/15		Fired three 100 lbs. from 4 pdr. & E.L. Right. Fuzes. No has burnous lying in Henna C. Continued on argot to Harra. Command shoot of G.2" hows on Sharbruck. Verr & black received. Enemy's trenches between × Wingg-berg & Schmelow. 1 Spl. reply.	JHB

T2134. Wt. W708-776. 500000. 4/15. Sir J. C. & S.

WAR DIARY
or
INTELLIGENCE SUMMARY.
(Erase heading not required.)

Army Form C. 2118.

Place	Date	Hour	Summary of Events and Information	Remarks and references to Appendices
	Sat 25/9/15		All guns in action. Exceptionally good fire towards dawn. No air observed, answered by the enemy. Extremely heavy firing audible from the south.	OMB

Army Form C. 2118.

WAR DIARY
or
INTELLIGENCE SUMMARY.
(Erase heading not required.)

5A Trench Mortar Battery

Instructions regarding War Diaries and Intelligence Summaries are contained in F. S. Regs., Part II. and the Staff Manual respectively. Title pages will be prepared in manuscript.

Place	Date	Hour	Summary of Events and Information	Remarks and references to Appendices
Lyshfield	19/5		Gas attack about 4 a.m. All positions opened gun fire into Vedruck ground do ever bridge 92 & approach	
F31-F35	20/5		Constructed dug out in the ter valley	
	21/5		Continued same	
	22/5		Cleaned ammunition & guns in store	
	23/5		Improved & took store near bridge 72	
	24/5		Buried experiment	
			W Spooner Capt R.F.A. O/C 3 ATM B	
	25/5		Butt & acces. shed 26. NN. B15. a.5.5.	

Army Form C. 2118.

WAR DIARY
or
INTELLIGENCE SUMMARY.
(Erase heading not required.)

34 Trench Mortar Battery

Place	Date	Hour	Summary of Events and Information	Remarks and references to Appendices
In the Field F.21-35.	26/12/15		Changed relief	
	27/12/15		Cleaned ammunition	
	28/12/15			
	29/12/15		Placed all bombs into watertight boxes for handing over	
	30/12/15		Inspection	
	31/12/15		Handed over to T.M.B's 4g 2t Div. at 6.30 pm	
	1/1/16		Moved into rest billets, cleaned up and billets	

M Donnell 2/Lt R.G.A.
O/c 34 T.M.B.

20,000 Sht. 27 N.W. 13 10 6.7.7

Army Form C. 2118

WAR DIARY
or
INTELLIGENCE SUMMARY
(Erase heading not required.)

3 4 Trench Mortar Battery

Place	Date	Hour	Summary of Events and Information	Remarks and references to Appendices
Sheffield	17/9/15		Making No 2 dug out waterproof; cleaning out reserve gun position of No 2 gun. Command Officers dug out.	
	18/9/15		Cleaning reserve gun dug out, entrained Officers dug out at night.	
	19/9/15		Had 3 Rounds in reply to enemy's mortars, (from No 3 gun) all activated their old hog probably aff: g 2 previous trenches from our trench or redoubt. Continued Officers dug out and retired telephone wires.	
	20/9/15		Completed roof of Officers dug out and repaired telephone wires. Enemy gun fire again opened fire on enemy left F33, we replied with 11 Rounds 2 Flight a short ranged which were damaged.	
	21/9/15		Quiet day; commenced servants dug out.	
	21/9/15		Fired 5 rounds 2 Heavy + 3 Light about 6.30pm in reply to enemies rum jar fire from No 3 gun & retaliated and 1 Heavy was a premature. Repaired inside of Officers dug out for RE's to renew. Henno sent note re newly given battle forts 17.	

N Demerara 24 RGA

21/9/15

No 34 T.M.B.

Army Form C. 2118.

WAR DIARY
or
INTELLIGENCE SUMMARY.
(Erase heading not required.)

Instructions regarding War Diaries and Intelligence Summaries are contained in F. S. Regs., Part II. and the Staff Manual respectively. Title pages will be prepared in manuscript.

Attached MGs Battn

Place	Date	Hour	Summary of Events and Information	Remarks and references to Appendices
2nd Field	5/7/15	10.00	Shot 1.2 & NW B19 + 5.65.	
	6/7/15		Contested any ad for Officers taking	
			Bait accounts. Centre registered	
	7/7/15			
	8/7/15			
	9/7/15		Commenced building dug out in same trench for telegraphists	
	10/7/15		Replenished new positions about two dumps of ammy (625 RDS)	
	11/7/15		Platoon gun in positions. Dugouts dug out.	
			W Donald Capt RGA	
			OC 24 TMB	
			J. Dickens Capt	
			49 (Div.) T.M.B's	

T2134. Wt. W708—776. 500000. 4/15. Sir J. C. & S.

49TH DIVISION

DIVL TRENCH MORTAR BATTERY
DEC 1916 - DEC 1918

1915 JLY — 1918 DEC

Vol 1

SECRET.

WAR DIARY.

OF

49th Div. Trench Mortar Battery

FOR

December 1916.

Army Form C. 2118.

WAR DIARY or INTELLIGENCE SUMMARY.

49th Divisional Trench Mortar Batteries

(Erase heading not required.)

Instructions regarding War Diaries and Intelligence Summaries are contained in F. S. Regs., Part II. and the Staff Manual respectively. Title pages will be prepared in manuscript.

Place	Date	Hour	Summary of Events and Information	Remarks and references to Appendices
FRANCE	1916. December		SHEET I	
HENU.	1st.		Captain J. Le Patre. 1/5 West Yorks. D.T.M.O. 49th Division is on leave England. Captain R.P. Walker OC V/49. T.M. Battery assumed temp: command of 49th Divisional Trench Mortar Batteries. Reference Maps: Sheet 57d & 51c 1/40000. Positions of Units. D.T.M.O. with 49th Divl Artillery HQ at CHATEAU HENU. W/49. Trench Mortar Battery at Fonquevillers. V/49. at Souastre, X & Z at Bienvillers, Y/49. at Fonquevillers. W/49 Trench Mortar Battery had 3 heavy mortars (9·45") in the line, and X, Y, & Z 49. Trench Mortar Batteries had 10 Medium 2" Mortars, all of which were situated in the sectors opposite MONCHY & GOMMECOURT. A light tramway was under construction in Fonquevillers for the heavy 9·45" Mortars of W/49 T.m Battery, and to day the personnel of W/49 & parts of V/49 with the assistance and ——— the supervision of R.Es worked on them.	L.B
	2nd.		W/49. Trench Mortar Battery still continued to work with the R.E.s on the light Railway. The personnel of the Medium Batteries is employed in renovating gun positions which are in a collapsible condition owing to the wet state of the weather. Brass Ares and joints used with 2" Trench Mortar for giving degrees right or left, were adjusted and tested to day; they proved very satisfactory for shooting on fixed targets. Return from 49th Division states "That all Medium Trench Mortar Batteries are, whilst in the line, to be under the tactical control of Artillery Group Commander, and under the D.T.M.O for all matters of administration.	L.B

WAR DIARY or INTELLIGENCE SUMMARY

Army Form C. 2118.

49th Divisional Trench Mortar Batteries

SHEET II

Place	Date	Hour	Summary of Events and Information	Remarks and references to Appendices
HENU	1916 December 3rd		Today 2" Trench Mortars cut wire in front of MONCHY at E.5.d.2.5.40. owing to the ground being exceedingly soft mend difficulty was experienced in getting the T.M. Beds to stand. The enemy manoeuvres were active. 2 new positions were found just in front and South of MONCHY.	L.E.B.
	4th.		Fatigue parties were detailed to dig and renovate positions. Work still in progress on the 9.45" Mortar Light Tramway.	L.E.B.
	5th.		Working parties renovating gun positions and cleaning up/passage ways to gun positions. Parties still continue to work on the light tramway.	L.E.B.
	6th.		Men of Medium Batteries employed in cleaning and sorting ammunition, overhauling guns etc.	L.E.B.
	7th.		Owing to the frost and thaw the gun pits etc were continually in a state of collapse, and needed constant attention. All men in the Medium detachment were rebuilding gun positions etc and repairing Bomb Stores.	L.E.B.
	9th.		Effective strength of T.M's to day :- X/49 Trench Mortar Battery 3 Officers 57 Other Ranks. W/49. 1 Officer 55 Other Ranks. X/49. 1 Officer 22 Other Ranks. Y/49. 2 Officers 21 Other Ranks. Z/49. 2 Officers 15 Other Ranks. Z/49 Trench Mortar Battery had a case of accidental injury to day :- 1.10640 and 3 men were gassed by fumes from a Charcoal Brazier, the fumes had not the slightest effect until the men left the dug out, they then fainted profusely and were taken to hospital. They returned in a few days.	L.E.B.

Army Form C. 2118.

WAR DIARY
or
INTELLIGENCE SUMMARY.   49th Divisional Trench Mortar Batteries.

(Erase heading not required.)

Instructions regarding War Diaries and Intelligence Summaries are contained in F.S. Regs., Part II. and the Staff Manual respectively. Title pages will be prepared in manuscript.

SHEET III

Place	Date	Hour	Summary of Events and Information	Remarks and references to Appendices
HENU	1915 December 9th		Battery came out in portion from the line and rest billets to HENU to be refitted with small box Respirators undergoing the 6 gas test under the supervision of the 49th Divisional Gas Officer. A New Stokes Mortar Rifle Mechanism for use with 2" T. Mortar was tested to-day by the Officer Commanding Y/49 Trench Mortar Battery. His opinion was that it would prove more satisfactory than the Bolt Pattern now Enfield Rifle Mechanism.	
	10th		20 men were transferred from 49th D.A.C. to 49th Trench Mortar Batteries in accordance with instructions issued by Staff Captain R.A 49th Division. These men proceeded to the line and helped with the parties in the construction of the Battery at Fonquevillers. 2/Lt J S Walton was transferred from Y/49 Trench Mortar Battery to 49th Trench Mortar Batteries. He took up his duties with X/49 T.M. Battery as second in command. O.C. Z/49 Battery 2/Lt Fisher Brown proceeded on leave to England.	
	11th		Instructions were issued by D.T.M.O for all Battery Commanders to report to Battalion Commander on their sector each day. 2 Rounds of 2" Bomb were fired by Y/49 Battery at Fonquevillers in retaliation to hostile trench mortar.	
	12th		Letter received from 49th Div to day stating "Although Trench mortars in the line are under the control of Artillery Group Commander, this must not interfere with the immediate action of	

Army Form C. 2118.

WAR DIARY
or
INTELLIGENCE SUMMARY. 49th Divisional Trench Mortar Batteries.

(Erase heading not required.)

Instructions regarding War Diaries and Intelligence Summaries are contained in F. S. Regs., Part II. and the Staff Manual respectively. Title pages will be prepared in manuscript.

SHEET IIII.

Place	Date	Hour	Summary of Events and Information	Remarks and references to Appendices
HENU	DEC 1916. 12th.		Trench Mortars.	
	13th.		The bombardment of the Monchy Salient was carried out at 11am to-day and the Heavy and Medium Trench Mortars W/49, Heavy Battery, & X/49 & Z/49 Medium Batteries in conjunction with the artillery bombarded the German Front Line. W/49 expended 30 rounds of 9·45" Ammunition X & Z/49 expended 100 Medium 2" Ammunition. The action of trench mortar ceased at 1·40 pm.	125
	14th.		The Third Army "BAB" Trench Code was circulated to V X Y Z T.M. Batteries for information and action. Retaliatory fire was carried out by Y/49 T.M. Battery & W/49 T.M. Battery.	125
	15th.		Y/49 T.M Battery expended 9 rounds 2" and V/49 T.M Battery expended 5 rounds 9·45" Ammunition. Orders were received by D.T.M.O. that Heavy 9·45" Mortars were only to fire at extreme range. The effective strength of to-day V/49 Trench Mortar Battery 3 Officers 66. OR W/49. 1 Officer 56 Other Ranks. X/49 Battery 2 Officers 22 Other Ranks. Y/49 Battery 2 Officers 23 Other Ranks. Z/49 Battery 2 Officers 29 Other Ranks. Total 10 Officers. 196 Other Ranks.	125
	16th.		Rather resembling Gun position and probably Ways Retaliation fire was carried out in response to Enemy Trench Mortar by W/49 Battery who fired 3 rounds 9·45" and Y/49 Battery who fired 17 rounds 2"; the enemy were silenced. In accordance with 49th Divisional Artillery Order No 151 of the 15th December 9 Officers were posted to 49th Divisional Trench Mortars from 49th Divl Artillery	125

T.134. W. W708—776. 500000. 4/15. Sir J. C. & S.

Army Form C. 2118.

WAR DIARY
or
INTELLIGENCE SUMMARY. A9th Divisional Trench Mortar Battery.

(Erase heading not required.)

SHEET V

Place	Date	Hour	Summary of Events and Information	Remarks and references to Appendices
HEBU	1916 December 16th		Units. Lieut Benson (MC) 2/Lt J Chilton. 2/Lt Beswick 2/Lt J Harvey 2/Lt Chippendale, 2/Lt Rhoee 2/Lt Hore 2/Lt Fowler 2/Lt Potter 2/Lt Buckton. These officers with the exception of 2/Lt Chilton X/49 Battery and 2/Lt AS Beswick W/49 T.M Battery, are at present detailed for duty with Field Batteries of the 49th Division.	E.15
	17th		Bombardments received gun and clean of ammunition stores. 5 2ind Bombs were expended by X/49 T.M Battery in retaliation to hostile minenwerfer.	E.15
	18th		Owing to the wet weather, Gun Positions were continually falling in. They needed constant attention.	E.25
	19th		Ordered would to day in connection with Bombardment of Enemy Trench Mortar positions on the 20th instt., to Battery Commanders. There was a slight activity of hostile mortars to-day and in retaliation to the W/49 T.M Battery expended 2 rounds 9.45" and 2/49 T.M Battery expended 8 rounds 2". Enemy guns were silenced.	E.C.
	20th		In conjunction with the artillery, Heavy and Medium (9.45"& 2") Trench Mortars bombarded Enemy Trench and Trench Mortar positions in front of COMMECOURT. 22 Rounds Heavy guns" were fired by Heavy Trench Mortars and 150 rounds were discharged by the 2" Medium Mortars. The enemy replied only during the 1st half hour. The Bombardment commenced at 8 am with.	

WAR DIARY or INTELLIGENCE SUMMARY

Army Form C. 2118.

49th Divisional Trench Mortar Batteries.

SHEET VI

Place	Date	Hour	Summary of Events and Information	Remarks and references to Appendices
HENU	1916 December 20th		Capt. Heavy Artillery and accident 12 men.	1.28
	21st		49th Divisional Trench Mortar Batteries were relieved by the 46th Divisional Trench Mortar Batteries in the morning. Heavy Batteries left all guns in Coys. area, and the Medium Batteries handed over their guns to 46th Division who had not an equivalent number. 49th D.T.M.O. proceeded from HENU to LUCHEUX (Map Sheet 51c) next area with 49th Divisional Artillery Headquarters. V/49, W/49, X/49, Y/49, Z/49, Trench Mortar Batteries proceeded from SOUASTRE to HALLOY with 49th Div. Artillery.	
HALLOY (SHEET 51c) N10.a.00	22nd		Batteries in rest billets at Halloy. Effective strength to day V/49. T.M. Battery 3 Off. 65 O.R. W/49 T.M Battery 2 Officers 68 men X/49. 2 Officers 28 men Y/49 T.M. Battery 2 Officers 29 Other Ranks Z/49 Battery 2 Officers 29 Other Ranks Total 11 Officers 219 Other Ranks.	1.28
	23rd		Routine work and fatigues for Town Major.	1.28
	24th		Wire from 7th Corps to Army States. Personnel of 49th Divisional Trench Mortar Batteries will proceed to 3rd Army School of Mortars on 10 January 1917 for instruction & training purposes. "B" that 2 N.C.O.s and 23 men from Siege Batteries RCA.	1.28
	25th		Notification from 49th Divisional "6" that 2 N.C.O.s and 23 men from Siege Batteries RCA in the field are detailed for duty with 49th Dvl Trench Mortar Batteries. These men will proceed to the school on the 10th January with the rest of the personnel.	1.28

WAR DIARY
or
INTELLIGENCE SUMMARY.

Army Form C. 2118.

49th Divisional Trench Mortar Battery

SHEET VII

Place	Date	Hour	Summary of Events and Information	Remarks and references to Appendices
HALLOY	1916 December 26th		Batteries informed of the importance of the Salvage of métale and artillery material especially on the forward area	
	27th		Routine Work and fatigues.	
	28th		Return rendered in accordance with VII Corps Routine Order. Shewing Other Ranks who have been in France for 9 months and over and have not had leave. V/49 Battery. 21 OR. W/49. 24 OR. X/49. 13 OR. Y/49. 12. OR. Z/49. 12.OR. Total 82 Other Ranks.	
	29th		Effective Strengths to day. V/49 T.M Battery 3 Officers 65 Other Ranks. W/49. 2 Officers 66 Other Ranks. X/49. Battery 2 Officers 37 Other Ranks. Y/49 Battery 2 Officers 2 Officers 26 Other Ranks. Z/49 Battery 2 Officers 29 Other Ranks. (11 Officers and 213 Other Ranks Total)	
	30th		N°. 205 Corporal J Brailsford V/49 Trench Mortar Battery & N°. 1150 Bombardier Batt A. Y/49 Trench Mortar were both presented with gallantry card from Divisional Commander for distinguished conduct in the field. whilst stretcher bearing at Beaumont Hamel on Nov. 15th-18th 1916. Captain J.G. Pelin Divisional Trench Mortar Officer returned from leave to day and reassumed duties from 3pm.	
	31st		Ten Other ranks proceeded to the 3rd Army School of Mortar at Ligny St Flochel for a course of training on the 2" Medium Trench Mortar. These men received from Artillery.	

WAR DIARY
or
INTELLIGENCE SUMMARY. 49th Divisional Trench Mortar Battery.

Army Form C. 2118.

SHEET: VIII

Place	Date	Hour	Summary of Events and Information	Remarks and references to Appendices
HALLOY.	December 1916. 31st		They travelled from DOULLENS to ST POL by 9.19 a.m. train arriving at ST POL about 2 p.m.	£3
			Total Rounds fired during Month of December. 55 Heavy 9·45" 389 Medium 2" " " " " " " " 1 Other Rand (Shell Short).
			" " " " amount of Casualties " " " "

Peters
Captain,
Commanding, 49th Divisional Trench Mortar Battery.

Secret

War Diaries

of

49th Divisional Trench Mortar Batteries

for

January 1917.

Vol 2

Army Form C. 2118.

WAR DIARY
or
INTELLIGENCE SUMMARY.

49th Divisional Trench Mortar Batteries

(Erase heading not required.)

Instructions regarding War Diaries and Intelligence Summaries are contained in F. S. Regs., Part II. and the Staff Manual respectively. Title pages will be prepared in manuscript.

Place	Date	Hour	Summary of Events and Information	Remarks and references to Appendices
FRANCE	1917 January 1st		The Divisional Trench Mortar Officer with the 49th Divisional Artillery Headquarters at LUCHEUX. The 49th Divisional Trench Mortar Batteries were at HALLOY in huts. All the HALLOY.	
			49 Divisional T.M's were on rest without area with Artillery. Reference maps sheet 57C and 57d. The T.M Batteries were employed whilst on the rest area on fatigues for Town Major and routine work and route marching.	
"	2nd		Routine Work and Fatigues.	
"	3rd		Route Marching Gun drill	
"	4th		Routine Work. An inspection was carried out to day by 906 R.A. 49th Div. at 2.30pm full T.M's	
"	5th		Routine Work. Physical drill	
"	6th		Batteries still employed on Fatigues &c. Gundrill	
"	7th		Routine Work & Fatigues. Gundrill	
"	8th		Routine Work & Fatigues. Gundrill	
"	9th		Routine Work & Fatigues. Gundrill	
"	10th		9 Officers and 145 Other Ranks, proceeded to 3rd Army School of Mortars for a whirling course. They reported at Doullens Station and proceeded to ST POL arriving during the afternoon. The party left behind were employed clearing up camp. &c	

T.131. Wt. W708-776. 500000. 4/16. Sir J. C. & S.

Army Form C. 2118.

WAR DIARY
or
INTELLIGENCE SUMMARY.
(Erase heading not required.)

29th Divisional Trench Mortar Batteries.

Place	Date	Hour	Summary of Events and Information	Remarks and references to Appendices
HALLOY	January 1917			
	11th		Batteries at School.	
	12th		Batteries at School.	
	13th		Batteries at School. Part of 29th Div Artillery relieved 30 Div Arty in the line at BASSEUX &	
	14th		Batteries still at School. 29 HQRA & 29 DTMO at LUCHEUX	
	15th		29th Div Artillery HQ and remainder of 29th Div Arty with exception of the party of	
	16th		Trench Mortars at Halloy moved to BAVINCOURT from LUCHEUX Trench Mortar Battery Commander came from ST POL to new area to reconnoitre 30th Divisional T.M position. Batteries still at School.	
	17th		Batteries at School. 29th DTMO and 30th DTMO preparing for relief.	
	18th		Batteries still at School.	
	19th		To night Batteries came from ST POL to BERLES & CROSVILLE by Motor Lorries and relieved 30th Div'l T.M's. V/29, Y/29 & Z/29 Batteries went to CROSVILLE (left sector) and W/29 and X/29 Batteries went to BERLES.	
	20th		Took over from 30th Div T.M's. 4 Heavy 9.45" Mortars and 12 Medium 2" Mortars. Co-ordinates of positions taken over and Co-ordinates of positions in use attached Appendices I & II	I & II
	21st		Batteries proceeded to the trenches and worked on position.	

Army Form C. 2118.

WAR DIARY
or
INTELLIGENCE SUMMARY.
(Erase heading not required.)

494 Divisional Trench Mortar Battery

Instructions regarding War Diaries and Intelligence Summaries are contained in F.S. Regs., Part II. and the Staff Manual respectively. Title pages will be prepared in manuscript.

Place	Date	Hour	Summary of Events and Information	Remarks and references to Appendices
FRANCE				
BAVINCOURT BERLES to COSVILLE	22nd		Battery with the assistance of R.E's are working on position which are in collapsed condition.	
	23rd		Battery occupying position. Very little Trench Mortar activity. Hostile was noticed about that fatigue.	
	24th		Battery occupying position.	
	25th		A return rendered to-day showed 68 Other Ranks in T.M's who have not had leave for 9 months & over. Battery in the line employed repairing positions.	
	26		Battery in the line repairing positions. No firing has been done yet. No firing	
	27		Battery still employed repairing position.	
	28		Battery employed finishing position. Operation Order issued to Day as per appendix III attached	III attached
	29		Heavies: 5 rounds were fired on W.23.a.90.55 from Heavy Mortar at W.23.a.73.59. These did great damage. (A premature occurred to-day on the 2" Mortar - consisting 1/160 and 1 Burma) 5 rounds were fired on W.29.6.10.40. These also did considerable damage. 5 rounds were fired from Dainville Railway at W.23.c.22.85 All three gave good results. 8 rounds were fired from Heavy Mortar 16.33.a.7.4. There are 3 blinds. Amongst these but not averaged State. Medium: to day Cat were: 40 rounds were fired from medium mortar at W.23.6.7.80 on to W.23.6.90.20 The wire was badly damaged. 80 rounds were fired from medium mortars at X.1.c.5.2 on to point X.7.6.40.70 and X.7.B.45.95. 39 rounds were fired from medium mortar at R.33.d.05.25. and X.2.6.95.30.15. Barrack wire	

T2134. Wt. W708-776. 500000. 4/15. Sir J.C. & S.

WAR DIARY
or
INTELLIGENCE SUMMARY.
(Erase heading not required.)

Army Form C. 2118.

49th Divisional Trench Mortar Battery.

Place	Date	Hour	Summary of Events and Information	Remarks and references to Appendices
FRANCE	Jany 1917			
BAVINCOURT	29		Fired from mortar at R.33.6.65.10 onto R.34.c.35.40. The men at all their posts	
BERLES au			is badly concealed. Hostile Trench mortar activity came from MARTINET'S WOOD. Heavy mortar 2 rounds to day J.08	
CROSVILLE	30		5 Rounds were fired from the heavy mortar at R.33.c.7.5 onto the enemy behind in R.33.c.	
			All rounds were effective, building material being observed to be blown into the air.	
			52 rounds were fired from medium mortar at X.1.c.5.2 onto wire at X.7.6.40.70 and	
			a lane was cut at the place. 52 rounds were fired from medium mortar at R.32.d.05.25	
			Good lanes were cut here at X.2.6.30.10 and X.2.6.50.30. Medium mortar at W.23.6.70.30 fired	
			on wire at W.23.6.90.70 shewing a good gap. 15 Rounds of Stokes Trench Mortar were fired	
			on R.33.a.90.50. These ran with difficulty owing to the binding of Rifle Mechanism	L.W
		31st	Only the Heavies fired to day. 15 rounds were fired from position W.23.a.7.B.59. onto front line	
			enemy trench between W.23.6.82.05 and W.24.a.15.45. These did considerable damage. State of	
			Ground was observed to be blown into the air. Enemy retaliated on No 1 position W.28.6.66.11	J.L.B
			with about H.2's and about 6 Rifle Grenades. The men have great difficulty owing to the cold weather	
			to the binding of Rifle mechanism.	
			Total Casualties :- 2. Total Rounds fired Heavies "9.45" - 48.	
			Not wounded by staff (Regulative) Medium 2" - 311	
			2" Bomb	

L. Bettis
Captain
Commanding 49th Divisional Trench Mortars

POSITIONS OF TRENCH MORTAR EMPLACEMENTS

49th Division.

The positions shewn below are laid with beds and are occupied.

RIGHT SECTOR

	9.45" Stationary Positions		
	No.1.	W.28.b.66.11.	
	No.2.	W.23.a.73.59.	
W/49 Bty:	9.45" Decauville Railway Positions.		
	No.B.	W.23.c.22.85.	) 1 Mounted
	No.C.	W.23.a.4.3.	) Heavy Mortar
	No.D.	W.17.c.99.01.	) on Railway.
	2" Positions		
X/49 Bty:	1. Neverending St	W.28.b.85.20.	
	2. Farnboro Rd	W.17.b.70.80.	

CENTRE SECTOR.

	2" Positions	
Y/49 Bty:	2.	X.1.c.5.2.

LEFT SECTOR.

	9.45" Positions.	
V/49 Bty:	No.4.	R.33.c.7.4.
	2" Positions	
Z/49 Bty:	1.	R.32.d.05.25.
	1.	R.33.d.20.55
	1.	R.33.d.40.50.
	1.	R.33.b.65.10.

※※※※※※※※※※※※※※※※※※※※※※※※※※※※※※※※※

SECRET

TRENCH MORTAR POSITIONS
49th DIVISION.

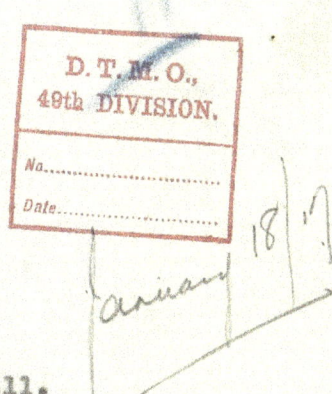
D.T.M.O., 49th DIVISION.
No..................
Date................

January 18/17

RIGHT SECTOR.

9.45" Stationary Positions.

No.1.	W.28.b.66.11.
No.2.	W.23.a.73.59.

9.45" Decauville Railway Positions.

No.A.	
No.A1.	
No.B.	W.23.c.22.85.
No.C.	W.25.a.4.3.
No.D.	W.17.c.99.01.
No.E.	

2" Mortar Positions.

2	Neverending Street	(W.28.b.85.20.
		(W.29.a.05.15.
1	Newark Street	W.29.a.85.45.) require
1		W.23.c.70.25.) repairing.
2	Farnboro Road	W.23.b.70.80.

CENTRE SECTOR

9.45" Positions.

NIL.

2" Mortar Positions

2	W.12.b.50.40.	- 1 good, 1 requires rebuilding.
1	W.12.b.8.7.	- requires rebuilding
2	X.1.c.5.2.	
2	X.1.c.5.2.	

LEFT SECTOR.

9.45" Positions.

No.3.	R.31.d.60.03.	Destroyed.
No.4.	R.33.c.7.4.	

2" Mortar Positions.

1	R.32.d.05.95.
1	R.33.d.20.55.
1	R.33.d.40.50.
2	R.33.b.85.10.
1	R.34.a.80.90.

SECRET

D.T.M.O.,
49th DIVISION.

No............
Date............

TRENCH MORTAR OPERATION ORDER NO: 10/53.

The 49th Divisional Trench Mortar Batteries will cut enemy wire as follows on January 29th 1917.

RIGHT SECTOR

X/49 T.M.Battery will cut wire between points :-

W.24.a.4.4.   and   W.24.a.8.8.
W.23.d.90.20. and   W.24.a.25.40.

W/49 T.M.Battery will fire on points :-

W.29.b.45.85.
W.29.b.10.40.
W.23.d.90.58.

CENTRE SECTOR

Y/49 T.M.Battery will cut wire on front between points :-

X.7.b.40.60.   X.1.d.80.80.

LEFT SECTOR.

Z/49 T.M.Battery will cut wire between points :-

R.34.c.20.25.   R.34.c.40.40.
also X.2.b.50.05.   X.2.b.75.30.

V/49 T.M.Battery will fire on points :-

X.2.b.55.15. & X.2.b.75.30.

Rounds per Medium Mortar ... 40.
Rounds per Heavy Mortar ... 5 on each point.

A report must be forwarded to reach this office by 6.pm. 29th instant, stating what wire has been cut.

Where the front is too large, lanes must be cut through the wire.

Captain,
Commanding, 49th Divisional Trench Mortars.

Issued at 6.pm.
Jany 28th/17.

Vol 3

SECRET.

WAR DIARY.

OF

Hqtrs Divl Trench Mortar Batteries

FOR

February 1917.

Army Form C. 2118.

WAR DIARY
or
INTELLIGENCE SUMMARY
(Erase heading not required.)

Sheet 1

49th Divisional Trench Mortar Batteries

Place	Date	Hour	Summary of Events and Information	Remarks and references to Appendices
BAVINCOURT BERLES & GROSVILLE	Feb 1st	—	The Divisional Trench Mortar Officer with the 49th Divisional Artillery Headquarters at BAVINCOURT. The 49th Divisional Trench Mortar Batteries were allocated as follows:— X/49 & W/49 in Billets at BERLES. V/49, Y/49 and Z/49 in Billets at GROSVILLE.	
	Feb 2		Wire was out at W.29.a.62.93 by Medium Battery. 8 rounds were fired. Other Batteries were strengthening positions and carrying up ammunition. Heavy Battery fired 6 rounds at point W.18.d.08.75. Shooting was erratic owing to wind. 8 rounds were fired on BLOCKHOUSE by Heavy Battery. Here did considerable damage Medium Battery fired 8 rounds killing 1 NCO and 2 men & an explosion occurred in Bomb Store. X/49 Battery and cleaning up 2 mortars. Batteries not firing were strengthening their positions.	
	3		No firing done today. Batteries repairing positions. 2/49 have 1 man wounded by shrapnel.	
FRANCE Shut. 51.e	4		In retaliation to enemy Trench Mortars, Heavy Battery fired from as an enemy cartwheels which were effective. Heavy mortars have now been removed to Pichaville Railway and is ready for action. A party of 1 NCO and 15 men of W/49 Battery have been employed all day in alteration of positions for Heavy mortars at W.28.c.66.11. New positions have been recommenced by V/49 in LANARK LANE.	

Army Form C. 2118.

WAR DIARY
or
INTELLIGENCE SUMMARY
(Erase heading not required.)

Sheet 11

Instructions regarding War Diaries and Intelligence Summaries are contained in F. S. Regs., Part II. and the Staff Manual respectively. Title Pages will be prepared in manuscript.

Place	Date	Hour	Summary of Events and Information	Remarks and references to Appendices
BAIZIEUX GRAVELLE 9/14/15/16	5 Feb.		No firing today. 2 Medium mortars in Limericks got into action. 1NCO and 15 men made good progress with Bomb store at W.22.a.59.01.	
Bayonne Trench Blauville 51c S.E.4 Edition 2A Vieux	6 Feb.		Heavy mortars fired 6 rounds in retaliation to enemy T.M's at point W.23.c.90.54 damage was not observed. 200 special cartridges have today been received from Third Army School of Mortars for trial and report. 1/49 have to-day had 2 men riflemen and 1 Bomb and 3 men wounded by enemy shell at point W.6.a.1.5	
	7 Feb.		No firing done today. Work on British continued.	
FRICHEUX 51c S.E. Edition 2C Vieux FRANCE Sheet 51c.	8 Feb.		Medium Battery fired 93 rounds on the following points. SALIENT on Dunton Road in R.34.c Trenches from X.3.b.9.9. to X.3.b.3.3, and wire at X.2.b.1/3 to X.2.b.80.35. (Rau Blockhouse) a large gap was made in the wire near the latter point. We have today shelled our front line with 5 g.s., no damage was done. In retaliation for our fire Enemy T.M's fired 7 Heavy and 30 Light T.M's on our trenches at W.23.c.80.50. Heavy Battery 1/49 fired 5 rounds on TROISMAISON & were effective. 3 Rounds also on X.2.b.95.25. reached their objective and were effective. 1/49 Heavy Battery fired 15 rounds on enemy earthworks at W.23.a.97.24. LANARK LANE continued.	
	9 Feb.		No firing today. Enemy very quiet. Work on positions on OAK St. and LIMERICK LANE	
	10 Feb.		Medium Battery at X.1.c.5.2. fired 104 rounds wire cutting, considerable damage done to wire, a lane cut through wire at X.1.d.35.20. A few enemy T.M Bombs were fired in retaliation to our fire. 1/49 Battery have moved Bomb store from Round and AID POST. BRETENCOURT to sunken Hollie at R.26.d.80.35.	

WAR DIARY or INTELLIGENCE SUMMARY

Army Form C. 2118.

Sheet. III

Place	Date	Hour	Summary of Events and Information	Remarks and references to Appendices
BAVINCOURT to BERLES to GROSVILLE	11 Feb		Scouts fired 8 rounds were cutting. 4 were effective 2 fell on Blairville and also considerable damage. Medium Battery fired 33 rounds on wire with good effect. Enemy Artillery retaliates to our fire but did no damage. Wire cleared after firing. Work will continue at Yarnborough Rd. Bomb carried from RAVINE to FARNBOROUGH ROAD. Work Dugout at Ravine proceeded with.	
BLAIRVILLE S.E. ¼ 51.a NW.2.A. ⅓ 57.c FICHEUX ST ¼ 51.c. 57.c Eastern 2.a	12 Feb		Medium mortars at X.1.c.5.2. fired 16 rounds with Temple Stokes during raid of 14 Y" Infantry Brigade on enemy Company Headquarters at X.Y. & 60 Y's mortars. About 200 Enemy shells fell on deep dugout lines and rear lines between FOREST STREET and FICHEUX STREET. These were painted with stars & yellow bands about 2" wide near fuze. S.A.A. cartridge filled with stars & salvo wrappers was found enclosing a report of this has been sent to XVIII Corps and 3rd Army School of Mortars.	
FRANCE Sheet 51.C	13 Feb		2/49 Battery fired 62 rounds wire cutting with good results. Heavy mortar fire 3 rounds on wire which failed to reach. Fire objects we put felt need to continue doing considerable damage. Considerable Enemy Artillery activity today but very little damage here. Batteries not firing were up army Battalio.	
	14 Feb		Medium Batteries fired Stormnos was cutting with good results. 1/49 Heavy Battery fired 3 rounds on wire as a covering fire for medium gunners. There was considerable enemy Artillery retaliation to our fire, and 1 medium mortar was buried in consequence. Sky is serves hit. Work was continued as previous Batteries not firing.	

WAR DIARY
INTELLIGENCE SUMMARY

Army Form C. 2118.

Sheet IV

Place	Date	Hour	Summary of Events and Information	Remarks and references to Appendices
Berles Bucquoy and Bucquoy	16th.		8 medium 2" Mortars have to-date been fitted with new adapter for 5 Rifle mechanism. Operation Orders received from 147 Infantry Brigade for a large raid to take place on 25 January. Z/49 fired 70 rounds on wire at R.34.c.35.45. marking a large gap in the wire. Considerable hostile artillery activity about our Rearline and support lines. Two enemy aeroplanes and 5 Observation Balloons were seen today near FICHEUX.	
BIENVILLERS SE 4 Souastre 2.A	17th.		Z/49 medium Battery fired 12 rounds on wire at R.34.c.25.45. Enemy TM's have been fairly active today. 50 to 6. Oilcan bombs falling in our trench.	
FICHEUX 52 S.2.3 Bailleulmont B80 MONCHIET May 57 c	18th.		Capt. Withycombe O.C. X/49 and 33 N.C.O's and men have to-day been transferred from BERLES to GROSVILLE to help to dig new gun pits for the forthcoming operations. Work on these is being continued through the night. 60 men were supplied by the infantry to help with these pits. X/14, Y/49 and Z/49. T.M. Batteries commencement wire cutting operations cutting in a desultory way so as not to excite the suspicion of the enemy. 2 lines each Battery were in action. 58 rounds were fired in all give results observed.	
	19th.		Wire cutting operations continued by the above 3 medium Batteries. Personnel of other Batteries helping with new gun positions. 49 rounds in all were fired today with good effect	

Army Form C. 2118.

WAR DIARY
or
INTELLIGENCE SUMMARY
(Erase heading not required.)

Sheet V

Instructions regarding War Diaries and Intelligence Summaries are contained in F.S. Regs., Part II. and the Staff Manual respectively. Title Pages will be prepared in manuscript.

Place	Date	Hour	Summary of Events and Information	Remarks and references to Appendices
WAILLY. BAVINCOURT. BERLES & GROSVILLE.	20th.		All wire cutting operations ceased owing to raid by 147 Inf Brigade being cancelled. Men of Y/49 attached to GROSVILLE for work on new position and put back in bed owl. Heavy and medium guns taken from new position and put back in bed owl. Heavy batteries retaliated to enemy shelling about our front line.	
Returned map BAPAUME 51c S.E. 4 Eastern 2A Issued map FICHEUX 51c S.E. Eastern 2A 1/10,000	21st.		Enemy T.M. very activity today. Heaves and mediums fired immediately and 5 mediums fired exploded.	
	22nd.		Heavy medium batteries retaliated to Enemy Artillery +T.M. fire, with 29 medium and 8 heavy rounds. 3 turns of 2/49 got in action in old position where positions opposite where collapsed through Thaw.	
FRANCE Sheet 51c	23rd.		Enemy Artillery and T.M's very act in today. Medium Heavy batteries retaliated with good effect. Enemy observed working on Blockhouse. Known chalk being thrown up at X 2. b. 5. 4. 10 men of 2/49 and 4 men of Y/49 filled with sandbags by Gas N.C.O.'s.	
	24th.		No firing today. Materials for positions carried up.	
	25th.		No operations today. A few rounds fired in retaliation to enemy T.M.'s	

Army Form C. 2118.

WAR DIARY
or
INTELLIGENCE SUMMARY

Sheet. VI

(Erase heading not required.)

Instructions regarding War Diaries and Intelligence Summaries are contained in F. S. Regs., Part II. and the Staff Manual respectively. Title Pages will be prepared in manuscript.

Place	Date	Hour	Summary of Events and Information	Remarks and references to Appendices
Bertles Granville & Beaucourt.	26th		Owing to 49" Divisional Artillery leaving XVIII th Corps area the 49" Division Trench Mortars are attached to the Line being 75. 58th Divisional Artillery, to whom all returns are rendered.	
	27th		Lieut Sarright O.C. V/49 T.M. Battery has today been admitted to hospital suffering from Trenchitis. Slight retaliation to Enemy T.M.s. Work on position continued.	
	28th		Very little firing done today. Front lines wh wired and cleared.	

Rowan (Capt)
49th Div T.M Btys

Vol 4

SECRET.

WAR DIARY.

OF

49th Divisional Trench Mortar Batteries.

FOR

March. 1917.

Army Form C. 2118.

WAR DIARY
or
INTELLIGENCE SUMMARY

MARCH 1917. Sheet 1.

(Erase heading not required.) 49th Division French Mortar Batteries

Instructions regarding War Diaries and Intelligence Summaries are contained in F. S. Regs., Part II. and the Staff Manual respectively. Title Pages will be prepared in manuscript.

Place	Date	Hour	Summary of Events and Information	Remarks and references to Appendices
GROSVILLE BERLES S. BASSEUX BAVINCOURT. Ref. maps. (LENS II.) 1/100,000	March 1st		The 49th Division Trench Mortar Batteries are still en route at BERLES & GROSVILLE. Divisional Trench Mortar Officer and Headquarters at BAVINCOURT. During the absence of Capt. E. Perry Capt. R.J. Walker V/49 T.M. Battery is acting D.T.M.O. and is billeted in BASSEUX.	S
	2.30 p	8 Woman heavy are fired in valedicts. 30 rounds medium fired in enemy line at R.34. a.3.4. Gun pits and dug outs cleared and repaired.	S
	2nd	Work on our pits etc. D.T.M.O. handed our all short maps. Gun positions etc to D.T.M.O. 58 Division at BASSEUX.	S
FICHEUX 6/a. S.E. & S.E. SW Edition 3.C. 1/10,000 RANSART 5/o. S.E. 3 & 4 Edition 3.C. 1/10,000	3rd	In accordance with orders received from G.H.Q., Guns and visitors were handed over to 58 Division. Several Heavy Batteries who reached our batteries at 9 a.m. One detachment per Battery remained on the fire until 4.30 pm. At 1 pm the remainder in accordance with Movement Order received from 149 Infantry Brigade, marched through LARBRET, LA BELLE VUE and POMMERA to HALLOY, arriving 5 pm. Detachments left on the line marched to HALLOY by same route arriving 11 pm. Batteries are billeted in huts at HALLOY (ref. maps LENS II.) 1/100,000	S
	4th	Batteries still in huts at HALLOY.	S
	5th	Batteries still in huts at HALLOY. Orders received from 149 Infantry Brigade for move on March 6th.	S
DOULLENS Reference maps (LENS II.) 1/100,000	6th	In accordance with movement Orders received yesterday, Batteries marched from HALLOY through GROUCHIES and AUTHIE to RANSART near DOULLENS (ref. maps LENS II.) arriving 1 pm. All Batteries billeted in farms.	P
		The Batteries marched to DOULLENS arriving 9 am. Entrained with 149 Infantry Brigade at 5 pm. Train left DOULLENS (4th Army area) at 6.30 pm and arrived at MERVILLE	S
MERVILLE ref. maps (HAZEBROOK) G.A.) 1/100,000	7/8		
	8th	(1st Army area) at 5 a.m. March 9th. Battns marched from station MERVILLE to LAGORGUE arriving 7am. All men quartered in billets.	S

WAR DIARY or INTELLIGENCE SUMMARY

Army Form C. 2118.

March 1914 Sheet II

49th Division Trench Mortar Battery

Place	Date	Hour	Summary of Events and Information	Remarks and references to Appendices
LABASSEE Rd M.Dp. HAZEBROUCK to RICHEBOURG ST. VAAST.	9th		Z/49 medium battery marched to RICHEBOURG arriving 9.30 am. All other batteries marched to LAVENTIE arriving 10 am. Guns and stores were taken over and relief of 56 Division taken over. The D.T.M.O. and Officer in LAVENTIE Battery mortar barracks comprised by 3 pm. W.Y. & X/ Batteries in LAVENTIE. Z Battery & men of Y Battery & 15 men of W Battery billeted at RICHEBOURG-ST. VAAST. 13 medium and 3 heavy mortars handed over by 56 Division. Teaching in stores taken. Y/49 2 officers 36 O.R. W/49 2 O.R. 6 O.R. X/49 3 officers 29 O.R. Y/49 2 officers 25 O.R. Z/49 2 officers 30 O.R. 3 ranks per French mortar officers are attached to battery in command.	I/S
RICHEBOURG LAVENTIE (Billets mapped) RICHEBOURG 36 S.W.3 Edition 7C x 10,000.	10th		No firing has been done today. Battery Commanders improved gun pits as enemy fire permitted.	I/S
	11th		No firing done today. Guns & ammunition cleaned. Gun pits cleared.	I/S
AUBERS 36 c/0.5.1 Edition 7c Jan 1916	12th		Medium battery fired 3 rounds in retaliation to enemy trench mortars fired without noise (?). Y/49 medium Battery fired 5 rounds on front line trench S.5. 6 ? 6.8 in retaliation with opposite other rounds from 8M6 Brigade R.F.A.(-). 8 rounds were fired at Barbette from 6 rounds on 15.11 & 10.10, 6 rounds on S.5 & 20.30 and 4 rounds at S.11 & 90.70 in retaliation to enemy trench mortars also dropped in the long burg large number of 'Barbette Barracks' engaged as enemy patrols are unable to cope with them (?). Enemy 7 M.G. shelled front line from S.10 to 5.20 Northwards.	I/S
	13th		Heavy trench mortars on S.11 & 92.62. Ruins of houses are let mercifully. Enemy amount of percussion on blown into air. 1 round & new 2 blue 260 rounds on S.S.a.45.15 (Ruin) complete corrugated iron and walls nearly concrete blown up. Between 2 & 3 pm Z/49 mortar fired 25 rounds from S.10 & 20.83 on S.10.6, 90.45 and S.10 & 6.6 45 (Central trench mortars and ammunition barrack) the last ground was a complete culvert attacking crater and putting gun pit on rest	I/S

WAR DIARY or INTELLIGENCE SUMMARY

Army Form C. 2118.

(Erase heading not required.)

Instructions regarding War Diaries and Intelligence Summaries are contained in F. S. Regs., Part II. and the Staff Manual respectively. Title Pages will be prepared in manuscript.

MARCH 1917 Sheet III

4th Canadian Siege Mortar Battery

Place	Date	Hour	Summary of Events and Information	Remarks and references to Appendices
LAVENTIE	March		Orders received from the 4th Brigade Headquarters of action to be taken on the LAVENTIE sector.	
RICHEBOURG	14	7.30 am	Batteries fired 10 rounds on S.5 a.45.15 ruins of house wall and timber on edge of crater. 30 rounds on S.11 a.92.62. Ruins observed. (Enfilading effect – shot was a result of gas set on the position yesterday a small ammunition dump seen to explode with intense flame)	/B
RICHEBOURG St. VAAST		9.30 am	Registration Burey was seen in the air. 10 rounds fired on S.5.a.60 by too much observing. 10 rounds on S.11 c.10.25 stones and fragments of house thrown up. At 2.0 pm 5 rounds fired on S.10 a.70.40 on the web.	
Section 7 c. 10,000		2.30 to 10.0	10 mortar fired on S.11 a.62.20 punch puts are now up. There were two minnies seen about 10.30 am. One other on by the gun about 5 yards the ruins about 10 yards rather explosive. Infantry reported Rosenberg (along short street PEPYS NOSE	/B
ROEUX St SE 1 Section 7 c. 100,000		7.30 am	MEDIUMS 10 rounds on FACE COUR D'AVRE (S.22.a.65.70) from mortar at S.22 a 00.20.	
			Effects: Rd. 1. Mortars at S.22. a.00.20 fired on drums. Good Periods S.22 a 08.96. 8 rounds and 8 mediums on DEMP T.M. (S.10.a.39.30) from Mortars at S.10.a.00.70	/B
		1.0 pm	Enemy Heavy Mortar fired from S.11. a.40.28 on POPE'S NOSE and vicinity also enemy BLITZ WOOD about 11 am. Heavy shelling fire on HUN STREET. Guns and ammunition recovered. Our Gun 1 shown much-needed Heavy Battery on HUN STREET to cease fire as trench was proceed on account of places.	
	15.		Team guns brought out of action. No horses secured.	/B
	16.		Effective Strength Of Batteries today M. 1/49 2 sb. 62 OR N/49-3 sb 68 OR N/49.3 sb. 68 OR X/49.3 sb. 22 OR 1/49.3 sb. 68 by Cast Rank 2/49 3 sb. 68. OR In accordance with orders received from O.C. 4th Division Heavy Mortars are brought down to ST VAAST DUMP to be taken away in lorries to the Canadian Division	

Army Form C. 2118.

WAR DIARY
or
INTELLIGENCE SUMMARY

(Erase heading not required.) 4Qᵗʰ Division Trench Mortar Batteries

March 1914 Sheet IV

Instructions regarding War Diaries and Intelligence Summaries are contained in F. S. Regs., Part II. and the Staff Manual respectively. Title Pages will be prepared in manuscript.

Place	Date	Hour	Summary of Events and Information	Remarks and references to Appendices
RICHEBOURG & LAVENTIE.	Mar 17		Medium held 38 rounds with good effect on S.22.a.65.90; S.22.a.80.42 & S.22.b.00.45 S.22.b.03.75; S.16.c.99.08 to S.22.b.00.86. Also 4 rounds in retaliation to Enemy T.M's on GRETCHEN TRENCH area 10.30.c.80.97. Lewis Vane Bombs fell in our front line about N.13.b.9.9. About 11 am. L Mortars opened TILLFLOY ST to attack as retaliation.	/S
Richebourg 36.S.W.3d Laventie 36. N.W.1 Bruton 7c. No. 610	18		"Indian" Battery fired 28 rounds on N.8.c.43.00. and N.8.d.30.80. in retaliation too to "numerously" firing on our front line at N.8.c.80.70.	/S
	19		Number of men who have not had leave for 1 year is 47. 2/49 Battery fired 22 rounds in front line trench S.22.c.55.68 to S.22.a.75.00 am. S.22.c.60.76. & S.22.c.80.62 with good effect and material early blown up. 2 rounds fired on S.22.a.65.70. Effect was lost. and carried out of target. 10 rounds fired on MITZI C.T. S.10.d.55.60 & S.10.d.66.45 with good effect. X 3/ Battery fired 23 rounds in retaliation to Enemy T.M's. on the following points:- trenches at M.30.c.80.95; Enemy Gun between N.19.a.51.N.18.a.34.35 and Enemy Gun at our M.24.c.85. Great M.R.4.25 fell on our support line from 300 yds back of gun position (M.24.c.87.70) Enemy T.M. fired on S TILLFLOY TRENCH. Bay (9.4.a.5") Stokes Mortar, Ammunition returned to 497.(WR) G.O.C.	/S
	20		No firing has been done to-day. Enemy activity- NIL.	/S
	21		2ⁿᵈ/L E.J.R. FOTTE (M. NORTH MIDLAND Brigade R.F.A.(T) X/49 T.M. Battery was wounded in the neck and back by our own M.R. Capt. R.H. NORLEDGE W/49 T.M. during his day succeeded to the command of X Mortar to assist on command of Kratching as D.T.M.O. 2/49 Battery fired 50 rounds on enemy first line and communication trenches on S.22.c. Here is a large amount of rubble in enemy line Enemy T.M. to shells on S.22.c.10.20 to S.22.a.30.60 in retaliation to our fire	/S

WAR DIARY or INTELLIGENCE SUMMARY

Army Form C. 2118.

March 1917 Sheet V

49th Division Trench Mortar Batteries

Place	Date	Hour	Summary of Events and Information	Remarks and references to Appendices
RICHEBOURG to LAVENTIE Rd. cross	March 22		Mortars in provision of Richebourg Day – 1B Medium 2", 6 LTMs with hostile silencers and 10 issued for Stokes silencers. 20 Rounds fired today by X & Y Batteries on Enemy trenches in retaliation to Enemy trench mortar fire. Slight Enemy T.M. & art. arty. activity.	/8
RICHEBOURG 36.S.W.3 Sq.yc Y/16 CCC	23		The effective strength of the Several Trench Mortar Batteries today is: X/49 2 Off, 61 O.R., Y/49 2 Off, 67 Other Ranks, X/49. 3 Off 30 O.R., Y/49 3 Off 27 O.R., Z/49 3 Off 38 O.R. 10 Rounds were fired by Z/49 on Southern arm of C.11.7.2.1, S.10.d.55.70 & S.10.d.65.45. Result fair.	/8
AUBERS 36.S.W.1 Fleurbaix 7c moc	24		19 Rounds fired by Z/49 on arc at S.10.d.85.85 & S.10.d.50.60 with good result. Enemy dumps of stopped Battery firing. Y/49 fired 80 rounds in retaliation to enemy TMs m M.30 & 67.70 and M.36 & 90.80 Enemy mortars ceased fire. Bombarded enemy T.M. pit on M.24.c.7.5 and At security during the morning.	/8
	25		Y/49 fired 12 rounds on enemy trenches about M.30.a. & 82.55 in retaliation to enemy TM. The 14 round was a premature killing one man and wounding 3 others severely and 1 slight and one man of the infantry who were in the area recently. Z/49 fired 30 rounds on S.16.a.60.40. Wire cutting. 6 came was cut in the air. X/49 fired 4 rounds in retaliation to enemy TM. on M.19.a.30.40. Enemy retaliated to our wire cutting operations with light shrapnel on S.15.c & 60.99. Bom activity on enemy T.M. activity about M.24.c.	/8
	26		A Court of enquiry was held at No D.T.M O3 Place LAVENTIE to enquire into the cause of the premature to the bore at No 5 of a 2" mortar 6" Y/49 T.M. Battery. Result – no firmness to the No 49 Division. No clue was found. X/49 Battery fired 4 rounds on M.H.C. 30.90 & M.19.c. 20.35 in retaliation to enemy wire bomb in the T.M's. Z/49 Battery fired 5 rounds on enemy wire S.16. & 60.70. Good front results.	/8

Army Form C. 2118.

WAR DIARY
or
INTELLIGENCE SUMMARY   March 1917   Sheet VI

(Erase heading not required.)   H.Q. Colonial Mortar Batteries

Instructions regarding War Diaries and Intelligence Summaries are contained in F. S. Regs., Part II. and the Staff Manual respectively. Title Pages will be prepared in manuscript.

Place	Date	Hour	Summary of Events and Information	Remarks and references to Appendices
LAVENTIE & RICHEBOURG	March 27		Medium Battery fired 9 rounds on wire at S.16.a.60.70. took fair results. 2/49 Battery fired 25 rounds on the following points:- S.22.c.90.50, S.22.d.10.40, S.22.d.10.40 in addition to Brindle T.M. firing on SHETLAND ROAD.	VS
Alt Maps 28A	28		Medium fired 10 rounds on wire at S.16.a.60.70. Enemy retaliated with trench mortars and pineapples on COCKSPUR STREET	VS
RICHEBOURG 36 S.W.3 Edition 7a 1/10,000	29		3 medium rounds on FARM COUR d'AVOUE. Enemy activity Nil.	VS
AUBERS 36 S.W.1 Edition 7a 1/10,000	30		Effective strength of Battens. 1/49. 2 Off. 61 O.R.; W/49 3 Off. 66. O.R.; X/49. 3 Off. 29. O.R. Y/49. 3 Off. 34 O.R; Z/49. 3 Off. 32 O.R. Gun. Perry E.E. no4152 Buried at M.22.c.45.60. Firing has been done today	VS
	31		No firing has been done today. Guns cleaned, platform renovated.	VS

W. Peters
Capt.
Commanding 49th Division Trench Mortar Batteries.

2449 Wt. W14957/M90 759,000 1/16 J.B.C. & A.   Forms/C.2118/12.

Secret.

Vol 5

War Diary
of
H.Q.ᵗ (w/c) 2nd Trench Mortar Battys.

April/17

Army Form C. 2118.

WAR DIARY
or
INTELLIGENCE SUMMARY

(Erase heading not required.)

April 1917   Sheet 1
49 & Division Trench Mortar Batteries

Place	Date	Hour	Summary of Events and Information	Remarks and references to Appendices
LAVENTIE & RICHEBOURG H.Meads 3 Eastern Ka 119,000 AUBERS 36.S.W.1 Eastern Ka 1/10,000	April 1		Z/49 T.M. Battery in action at RITCHEBOURG. Y, X, V, & W. being also in action at LAVENTIE. The Divisional Trench Mortar Officers & Headquarters also in LAVENTIE. Others will administer fire X & Y/49 T.M. Batteries for ten days intensive operations with a view to assisting the infantry. There were registered and positions reconnoitred today. Z/49 Medium Battery fired 8 rounds on Enemy front line from S.22.c.80.35 to S.22.a.90.25 and in aid of Y/49 fired 25 rounds from M.24.d.06.85 on Tommy wire and front line at M.24.d.H.0.80 to M.24.d.75.35, 9 rounds from M.24 to 60.90. 31 rounds from N.13.c.25.40, 16 rounds from N.14.a.10.58. 3 rounds from N.8.c.35.15 in accordance with wire cutting scheme. Y/49 medium Battery fired 5 rounds from M.29 F.92.15 and 34 from M.29 F.92.15 on the shot of positions. Enemy reply with artillery and Trench Mortars but no damage was done to our positions.	(Sgd)
	2		Z/49 Medium Battery fired 30 rounds from S.22.c.16.35 on enemy front line in retaliation to Enemy T.M. which fell on our front line. 4/49 medium Battery fired 127 rounds and X/49 32 rounds were cutting as per scheme X/49 medium Battery had 1 Emplacement which remained registered Slightly. Very heavy shelling by Enemy with 77mm, + 2" & 5.9". Got detail on hour in retaliation to rifle fire was burnt stores were thrown in and position at M.35 F.87.75 was damaged.	(Sgd)
	3		Z/49 Medium Battery fired 15 rounds from S.23.c.32.18 in retaliation to Enemy T.M. Y/49 medium Battery fired 90 rounds and X/49 — 96 rounds on special wire cutting positions Enemy shelled with 130 rounds 4.2 c.guns at M.29 & S0.32. Enemy and Ours still along front line in front of guns at M.25. F.90.68. Guns at S.5.a.96.23 was suspected to Enemy Fire from medium T.M, 5.9. and 77mm and our retirement Forced to leave the gun.	(Sgd)
	4		Y/49, X/49 medium Batteries continued wire cutting. Y/49 were being fired on Enemy wire. Enemy retaliated with 5.9. 4.2. & 77mm. But no damage done to our Batteries Stores or mortars today :— 12 medium 2" mortars in front of his Divisional front	(Sgd)

2449 Wt. W14957/M90 750,000 9/16 J.B.C. & A. Forms/C.2118/12.

WAR DIARY or INTELLIGENCE SUMMARY

Army Form C. 2118.

Sheet II
April 1917

49th Division French Mortar Batteries

Place	Date	Hour	Summary of Events and Information	Remarks and references to Appendices
LAVENTIE & RICHEBOURG Rd. maps 36 Sw 3 Edition 8a 1/10,000	April 5		Y/49 & X/49 Medium Batteries expended 193 rounds wire-cutting and 2/49 Battery 4 rounds in eradication to Enemy Church Mortars. Enemy retaliated to our fire with Artillery and T.M.'s but no damage was done. 1 Gunner was slightly wounded by shell fire. 2/49 Medium Battery had a prematic slightly wounding 2 Gunners.	
RICHEBOURG	6		Effective strength of Batteries today:- Y/49 2 ℔ 6 O.R. W/49 3 ℔ 6 6 O.R. X/49 3 ℔ 30 O.R. Y/49 3 ℔ 23 O.R. Z/49 3 ℔ 32 O.R. X/49 Medium Mortar fired 55 rounds on M. 24.d. 30.15. N.19.a. 30.70 & April 8 daylight line. Y/49 Medium Mortar fired 110 rounds on M.30.a. 30.25. M.36.c. 15-25. & M.5.L.45.15. All wire-cutting. Enemy retaliated heavily with Artillery and T.M.s on our front line near CHURCH ROAD. One of our Detachment wounded by rifle grenade.	
AUBERS & Edition 8a 1/10,000	7		Medium Batteries fired 177 rounds wire-cutting on the following points:- M.30.B 30.60 M.24.d. 75.45, M.19.a.30.45 about line & French Tramway N.19.a.45.85, wire front line near tramway about N.8.a.30.10, 3.5. & 77.6.5.5. & 75.60, M.30.a.40.15-35 M.30.c.52-72 M.30.a. & 4. to M.30.a. 80.42. Enemy retaliated with slight T.M. and artillery fire. 1 N.C.O. was killed by enemy shrapnel.	
	8		138 rounds over fired by Medium Batteries wire-cutting on the following points:- M.30.a.65.00, M.30.a.80.45, M.20.a.98.45, M.30.a.70.45 & M.30.a.98.45, M.24.a.75.45 M.19.a.50.85, front line French and tramway N.14.a.80.40. One poiluon M.29 & 79.52 was riddled with 77 mm. Several Enemy grenatowerfrs fell on our line during the morning.	
	9		133 Medium rounds expended on wire cutting of various of following points the following:- M.19.a.15.60, Launch tramway & front line N.13.c.90.30 & N.13.a.20.40, N.14.c.70.45 M.30.a.38.55 & S.5. & 85. #8 Enemy retaliated with whizz bangs 5.95, 77 mm, 4-25 rifle grenades and T.M.s	

Army Form C. 2118.

WAR DIARY
or
INTELLIGENCE SUMMARY

(Erase heading not required.)

Sheet III
April 1917.
39th Division Trench Mortar Batteries

Instructions regarding War Diaries and Intelligence Summaries are contained in F.S. Regs., Part II. and the Staff Manual respectively. Title Pages will be prepared in manuscript.

Place	Date	Hour	Summary of Events and Information	Remarks and references to Appendices
LAVENTIE	April 10		38 Rounds fired by X/49 & 63 by Y/49 Medium Batteries wire cutting on the following points:— Distance N.19.a.70.95 & N.19.a.40.80 & Support Line N.13.a.30.28 & N.14.a.80.40	
RICHEBOURG ST. VAAST			2/49 Medium Battery fired 23 rounds in retaliation to Enemy T.M.s with good effect. No real wire cashed out at 10.25pm.	
RICHEBOURG St. S.W.3 Edition 8a 10,000	11		Battery fired 9 rounds on crater at M.30.c.40.02 and M.30.a.45.15. Enemy retaliated heavily to Mortar firing on wire. Medium Battery fired 100 rounds on the following areas M.30.a.85, M.30.a.6.4, front line and wire M.30.a.40.15 and M.30.c.52.90, Trench line and Tramway M.19.a.53.92 front line and Tramway N.14.a.80.40. All with good effect. Enemy retaliated with 77mm L.F. Gun and whizz-bangs.	
AUBERS 36. S.W.I Edition 8a 10,000	12		Fired 16 of Mortars, 12 Mediums, Heavies NIL. 23 rounds Medium fired on S.22.c.60.50 Enemy wire S.22.c.50.60 and N.19.a.90.50 in retaliation to Enemy Medium T.M. falling on our line about M.24.a.20.60 and S.22.c.20.33. Enemy T.M. replied with salvos from H.2 Battery near S.21 & S.9.20.	
	13		Medium firing 16 X/49 2 Bn. 57 O.R. Y/49 3 Bn. 64 O.R. X/49 2 Bn. 29 O.R. Y/49 3 Bn. 32 O.R. Y/49 3 Bn. 33 O.R. V/49 Bn. P.H.P.b. X/49 evacuated to England wounded. 1 medium rounds were fired on mines at M.30.a.50.50 in arrangement with Scrimshaw Company 36 rounds on wire S.22.c.50.75. Enemy retaliated with H.2 R.E. and 4 Vanus Bons. Slight Enemy T.M. activity.	
	14		Medium Battery fired 18 rounds on suspected Machine gun emplacement N.19.c.70.95. Large bursts of cordite were blown up. Enemy retaliated with H.2 H.E. Dupauquissart Church 50 rounds were fired by trench medium mortars on our own wires ERITH C.T.	
	15		13 Medium mortar fired today on Enemy Trench and wire at S.16.a.65.50 with his results. One round was a dissemal and our position temporarily out of action. No image of TOURNAI & VALENCIENNES 1/100,000 drawn today	

Army Form C. 2118.

WAR DIARY or INTELLIGENCE SUMMARY

(Erase heading not required.)

40" Division Trench Mortar Batteries   Sheet IV   April 1917

Instructions regarding War Diaries and Intelligence Summaries are contained in F. S. Regs., Part II. and the Staff Manual respectively. Title Pages will be prepared in manuscript.

Place	Date	Hour	Summary of Events and Information	Remarks and references to Appendices
RICHEBOURG & LAVENTIE	April 16		25 medium rounds fired on Enemy line and wire at S.16.a.85.95 and the LOZENGE in N.19.a. in retaliation to Enemy T.M. Enemy retaliated with light barrage.	[sig]
Rd. major	17		15" medium rounds fired on N.19.c.30.95 and N.19.c.30.95; C.T. N.19.c.0.50 with good results. About 15 hostile T.M. between 6p.m. & 7p.m. in ERITH TRENCH	[sig]
RICHEBOURG 36. Jur. 3 Eclair Ba 40.000	18		16 medium rounds on Enemy front line in S.10.d in retaliation to enemy T.M. 30 rounds hostile T.M. fired on our left front line trench about M.24.f.&.J.	[sig]
	19		Retaliation: 9 medium rounds on N.19.a.60.90. Shells M.T.M. shelled ERITH & ELGIN Trench. H.T.M. from District shelled our Pride line on M.24.F.6. 40 L.T.M. fire on support line between MASSELOT & WANGERIE Trenches. Enemy trench mortars destroyed positions N.14-1	[sig]
BUBERS & LW Eclair Ba 40.000	20		Effective strength: Craters x/49.2.04. 57 O.R. W/49.30.4. 60 O.R. X/49.2.54. 29 O.R. Y/49.3.4. 22 O.R. Z/49.3.04. 32 O.R. Total 13 Offs. 210 O.R. Z/49 medium Battery fired 22 rounds on trench junctions S.11.c.05.75 in retaliation to hostile T.M. which fell on our line about S.16.t.30.60	[sig]
	21		10 medium rounds expended in retaliation on trench junction S.11.c.05.75 for a burst T.M. which fell about S.10.5. 43 rounds medium @ 2.60 compressed pens destroyed by Enemy Shell fire	[sig]
	22		Z/49 medium Battery fired 10 rounds from S.31.f.99.38 on trench at S.22.d.60.00 2 rounds hostile T.M. on S.22.c.20.30 between 7 & 8am. 10 rounds T.M. fired on our front line near ELGIN C.T. from M.T.M. in front of DISTILLERY on N.19.c. 2 or 3 hostile T.M. were fired into our trenches about M.25.t.98.90.	[sig]
	23		Hostile T.M. fired 10 rounds about 2am. on front line in front of FAUQUISSART. Our mortars at M.24.d.60.73 completely destroyed. 10 hostile T.M. fell between ERITH & ELGIN trenches. Enemy Mortar firing from ILES MOTTES FARM.	[sig]

WAR DIARY or INTELLIGENCE SUMMARY

Army Form C. 2118.

Sheet V

April 1917

2nd Division Trench Mortar Batteries

Place	Date	Hour	Summary of Events and Information	Remarks and references to Appendices
LAVENTIE & RICHEBOURG	April 24		No firing has been done today. Enemy battery - M.L. - a hostile balloon causing conversation indicates was located in M.2 wood N.W. of MARQUILLIES street T.17.c.6.2.	A/W
RICHEBOURG Ref. map 36 S.W. 3 Edition 8a 1/10,000	25		Retaliation - 8 medium rounds on S.10.d. 55.65, 12 medium rounds on S.10.d. 20.80. X/49 Medium Battery fired 8 rounds on TRIVELET — registering; 7 hostile T.M. fell near button S.10.d. 20.80. Seven of our retaliation.	A/W
	26		2 rounds medium fired from M.24.A.6.0. 43 on enemy trenches, 23 hostile L.T.M. on our front line. Enemy works — long Battery located at N.31.C.30.45.	A/W
AUBERS 36. S.W. 3 Edition 8a 1/10,000	27		Effective strength — V/49 2.M. 57 O.R. X/49 3.M. 60 O.R. X/49 3.M. 29 O.R. Y/49 3.M. 20 O.R. Z/49 3.M. 340 O.R. 4 rounds fired by X/49 Medium Battery onto TRIVELET. About 65 Enemy Medium T.M.'s fell between ELGIN & ERITH from 5.30 p.m. to 5.45 p.m.	A/W
	28		5 rounds fired by X/49 from N.14.B.00.15 on hostile working party. 5 rounds Enemy T.M. on ERITH C.T. at 5 p.m.	A/W
	29		Z/49 Medium Battery fired 15 rounds on french junction at S.10.d.55.60. X/49 Medium Battery fired 5 rounds on BERTHA TRENCH. Enemy fired 4 rounds T.M. on S.10.5.	A/W
	30		Z/49 Medium Battery fired 15 rounds on trench junction S.10.d.55.60 in retaliation to 3 hostile T.M. fired on LANSDOWNE C.T.	A/W

A.J. Walker Capt. Canada
49th W.A. T.M. Bgde.

956

Confidential

War Diary
of
49th Can Trench Mortar Batteries
for
Month of May 1917

Original

WAR DIARY or INTELLIGENCE SUMMARY

Army Form C. 2118.

May 1917 Sheet 1

49th Division Trench Mortar Batteries

(Erase heading not required.)

Instructions regarding War Diaries and Intelligence Summaries are contained in F.S. Regs., Part II. and the Staff Manual respectively. Title pages will be prepared in manuscript.

Place	Date	Hour	Summary of Events and Information	Remarks and references to Appendices
LAVENTIE & RICHEBOURG	May 1		N.X.Y. Batteries are all billeted in LAVENTIE with detachments on the line. W & Z are billeted at RICHEBOURG. Divisional Trench Mortar Officer is still in LAVENTIE	
	2		Heavy Battery to day fired 2 rounds registering	
RICHEBOURG 161 Marks RICHEBOURG 36 SO 3 Millar 80	3		No firing done to day. Enemy fired about 12 rounds M.T.M. on our front line from Mortar at N.19.c & 40.01. (When firing the last round this gun appeared by flash flaming above the road) 1st Howitzer was located firing from (1) N.33.a.6.5.5 and (2) N.33.a.6.0.15	
VAUBETS 36 SO 1 Hudson Sq W. C. LOD	4		10 rounds were fired by Heavy Mortar on to Enemy Mortar in BOIS DE BIEZ trench battery fired 26 on Trench junction S.10.d.55.60 and S.10.d.70.40 in retaliation to enemy T.M. falling round LANSDOWNE C.T.	
N10,000	5		9 Medium rounds were fired on DEVILS JUMP & BERTHA S.T. Signal Sqn. 12 Medium rounds on Enemy mens wire at N.14.c.9.5. and 12 Medium rounds on N13.d.9.0.7.5 (Enemy retaliated with 100 rounds 3 Medium Rounds registering on Enemy Trench and 5 rounds on Enemy wire N.14.a.9.5. Enemy T.M. activity nil.	
	6		20 Medium rounds on Enemy wire between N.14.a.9.0.5.0 and N.14.a.9.5.5. wire was entirely cut 25 Medium rounds on N.14.b.30.90 and N.14.a.25.50 with good results Enemy T.M. activity - NIL	
	7		12 Medium rounds on N.13.d.75.55 with good effect. Enemy T.M. activity - NIL 5 been detailed to attend 1st Army Rest Camp 20 Medium rounds fired on Machine Gun emplacements S.5.b.72.97 and M.35.d.85.17 Heavy medium was fired on Enemy retaliated to the above firing with Vans bombs during a raid by the Infantry. Medium battery fired 123 rounds on the following points. BERTHA TRENCH, N19.a.30.55	

WAR DIARY
or
INTELLIGENCE SUMMARY.
(Erase heading not required.)

Army Form C. 2118.

May 1917 Sheet II
49th Division Trench Mortar Batteries

Place	Date	Hour	Summary of Events and Information	Remarks and references to Appendices
LAVENTIE & RICHEBOURG Rt. Major	May 7		N19.a.25.75 N19.a.30.65. N.19.a.30.70. N19.a.40.75. N19.a.45.85. During this raid Enemy Range opened batn. widely about 3 minutes after ours, the majority of the shells bursting from 30 to 50 yards behind our front line with only a few just short of the parapet. After about 10 minutes this ceased and a few fell in the neighbourhood of medium mortar position N13 B.45.99 and N14.a.48.85 and only a few fell down PICANTIN C.T.	
RICHEBOURG 36.S.S.3 Edition 5a.	8		No firing has been done to-day by Medium Batteries. Heavy battery fired 10 rounds on S3.c.30.30 and M35.d.90.35 during operation. Sergt J.C. Lees 1/5 West Yorks DT M B was admitted to Hospital (sick) Capt R.F. Wallis V/49 T.M.B. assumed command	
AUBERS 36.S.S.1 Edition 5a.	9		10 Medium rounds on C.T. at S10.d.70.30 and 10 Medium rounds on junction of C.T. and Support line at S16.b.00.70 (Unobserved) No Enemy activity of T.M.s	
	10		Heavy battery fired 3 rounds on M36.a.60.10 and M36.a.60 in retaliation to Enemy T.M. "Bull" Enemy T.M. crater fire. 2 Heavy rounds on M36.c.25.60 medium batteries fired 7 rounds on M30.c.65.50 and N19.a.8.5 in retaliation to Enemy L.T.M. falling on N29.b.6.20. Enemy scaled Heavy Mortars at M29.c.93.10 rounds about 4.0 - 4.25 a new Rifle Midden no had been used with N.T.M's but these pieces were investigated, damaged, and reinforces after the first two pieces were At R. Rains O.C. X/49 Battery has to-day proceeded to join the R.F.C.	
	11		Effective Strength of Batteries to-day is :- V/49 2 Off. 56 O.R. W/49 3 Off. 57 O.R. X/49 2 Off. 28 O.R. Y/49 3 Off. 22 O.R. Z/49 2 Off. 56 O.R. Y/49 Medium fired 3 rounds in retaliation to 3 T.M. falling on our line at M30.d.48.30 X/49 Medium battery fired 9 rounds on Enemy M.G. Emplacement N19.a.35.40 large pieces of "concrete were blown up.	

A 5834 Wt. W4973/M687 750,000 8/16 D.D. & L. Ltd. Forms/C.2118/13.

Army Form C. 2118.

WAR DIARY
or
INTELLIGENCE SUMMARY.
(Erase heading not required.)

May 1917 Sheet 1
49th Division Trench Mortar Batteries

Instructions regarding War Diaries and Intelligence Summaries are contained in F. S. Regs., Part II. and the Staff Manual respectively. Title pages will be prepared in manuscript.

Place	Date	Hour	Summary of Events and Information	Remarks and references to Appendices
LAVENTIE & RICHEBOURG Map Ref:	May 12		45 Medium rounds fired at 3.22 c 85.10 kept out in opp enemy retaliated with 10 light H.E. shell on ROPE ST. Enemy whizz-bang battery from keep at N.1 b 25.40 was very active.	
RICHEBOURG Map Ref: Sheet 3 Edition 3a	13		Carried heavy firing in retaliation to Enemy's medium T.M. Medium Battery fired 7 rounds on firing line about N14 b 45.11 Retaliation to Enemy T.M. firing on out post line N of PICANTIN AVENUE from IRMAS ELEPHANT at N14 b 55.11.	
	14		35 Medium rounds fired on Enemy wire from 3.23 b 00.45 to 3.23 b 10.60. Several pieces of wire thrown in the air. As the target was behind a building observation was not possible. Enemy T.M. activity Nil.	
36 SW 1 Edition 3a do do	15		10 Rounds Heavy wire fired at trenches from 35 b 40 to 35 b 75.56 with good results all falling in enemy front line. 3 rounds Heavy on Enemy T.M. (FOX) at 5 6 d 90.30 Boards and timber were flung into the air and considerable damage done. 2/49 Medium Battery fired 15 rounds in the following points. Wire at 3.23 c 80.35, M.G. C.T. wire at 3.16 a 55.80 wire at 3.23 c 80.35, SALAD C.T. at 3.16 b 10.70 and MITZI C.T. all with good effect. Wire was badly damaged to rounds Heavy fired on Enemy front line between 36.1 45.00 and 35 b 70.40 with good results, large quantities of trench material thrown up to 2 rounds Heavy on Enemy front line M.36 a 70.00 2 out-outs and tremendous amount of material thrown into the air. amongst which came the body of a German. Several Light Enemy T.M. fell on NEUVE CHAPELLE and front line at M.35 d 65.30 in retaliation to out Heavy hostility. The enemy was using a small Stokes mortar. Firing light. The large Gun very active going well behind our gun in DEAD HORSE COPSE.	

Army Form C. 2118.

WAR DIARY
or
INTELLIGENCE SUMMARY.
(Erase heading not required.)

May 1917   Sheet II
49th Division Trench Mortar Battery

Place	Date	Hour	Summary of Events and Information	Remarks and references to Appendices
LAVENTIE & RICHEBOURG Ref Map RICHEBOURG 36 SW 3 Bastion S.a 110.000 AUBERS 36 NW Battle Hqrs there on.	May 1917 16		Heavy Mortar fired 12 rounds on Enemy Trenches from S.5.d 40.45 to 55.45 and also very good results. Enemy Mortar Fox at S.5.a 90.30. Replied with 11 rounds falling to left and right of it S.5.6 85.65 but caused no retaliation from our Heavy Mortar. 10 rounds Heavy fired on Enemy Trenches from S.5.6 70.45 to 85.6 55.72. Trough given finally corrugated iron. No blown up and considerable damage done to Enemy 15 rounds Heavy were fired on Enemy Trench mortar damage was done. Corrugated iron blown up. A dug-out was set on fire. 2/49 Medium Battery fired 10 rounds on the following points - North of S.7 and subsonk S.10.d 60.45 in retaliation to 2 hostile T.M. bombs on S.10.d 15.50 S.10.c 90.65 and d.90.15.00. All with good results. One round won a known in 1/49 Medium T.M. fired 14 rounds on front line at M.35.d 87.92 and M.35.a 65.20 (in connection with H.T.M.) 3 Enemy vans bombs fell on CHATEAU redoubt. 20 hostile 4.25 were fired at BALUSHI TRENCH about 10.17 hrs and 10 a.m. We fired at our Hostile at M.29.a.97.10. many of these fell in above trenches of the gun. Some good irritation on NEW CUT ALLEY and this fired heavy on CHURCH ROAD in retaliation. 6 7/49 Battery fell	
	17		17 round Heavy fired on trenches between S.5.6 75.55 and M.35.a 80.10. were 10.105 were used, doing very little damage. The enemy keeping lively on firing. 8 rounds Heavy were fired on Trench Junction M.36.a.15.70 and M.36.a.75. large amount of Revetting material and kitch filth blown up. Also finished which had been a small dug-out. 10 rounds Heavy on Enemy trenches from S.5.a 20.45 to S.5.d 50.65. A dug-out was blown in and	

WAR DIARY or INTELLIGENCE SUMMARY.

Army Form C. 2118.

May 1917   Ref Y   49th Division Trench Mortars in Kliws

Place	Date	Hour	Summary of Events and Information	Remarks and references to Appendices
LAVENTIE & RICHEBOURG Ref Maps 36 SW 3 Edition No 1B 1/10,000 AUBERS 36 CSE 1 Edition 8a 1/10,000	May 17	20 h	Considerable damage done to Lincoln & Range Heavy was fired in retaliation to Enemy M.T.M. 1 round a Bloom that others fell nr but not on target. 4/49 Medium Battery fired 7 rounds on M36 c 05.20, M36 d 86.30 and M36 d 80.10 with good results. 2/49 fired 61 rounds with entries on S23 c 85.30, S22 c 75.40 and S20 a 70.75. Two Enemy batteries fired heavily, shelled guns at M29 c 93.10 with 4.2s between 60 and 70 rounds being fired. Enemy M.T.M. from the wood probably about S5 d 95.40 teased on our retaliation. Effective strength of batteries today is X/49 5 Off, S6 O.R. V/49 3 Off, 57 OR. Y/49 2 Off, 28 OR. 4/49 3 Off, 22 OR. 2/49 2 Off, 25 OR. 17 rounds were fired by Heavy Mortar on Aubers from S5 b 7.95 to M35 c 9.8 to Indian Khud, the others gave good results. 16 rounds were fired from Heavy Mortars on Enemy trenches from S23 d 0.45 to S5 d S0.85. All rounds were observed to fall in Enemy lines. Considerable damage caused and Bosch would be driven up. 15 Medium rounds on Enemy T.M. from L00 about S21 d 20.30. Silenced T.M. and then section of trench tramway in the air 16 medium rounds were at S28 c 50.60, 8 medium rounds on wire at S10 d 40.80 and 4 rounds on wire at S10 a 40.50 all with good results. 4/49 Medium Battery fired 3 rounds on N19 a 25.40 in retaliation to Enemy Van Bomb. Enemy shelled guns at M35 c 55.29 with 4.2s. Two shells falling within 10 yards of gun. 2 Enemy M.T.M. fell by the CHATEAU in NEUVE CHAPELLE. About 5 Enemy Van Bombs fell on our front line near M13 c 10.22 to which X/49 Allahabad Enemy shelled in the neighbourhood of NEW PUTALLEY and BALUCHI TRENCH.	

Army Form C. 2118.

WAR DIARY
or
INTELLIGENCE SUMMARY.
(Erase heading not required.)

May 1917 Sheet VI
49th Division Trench Mortar Batteries

Place	Date	Hour	Summary of Events and Information	Remarks and references to Appendices
LAVENTIE & RICHEBOURG Ref Map 36.S.W.3 Edition 8a 1/10,000	May 19		6 Heavy rounds were fired on N.19.a.6.7. in retaliation to Enemy Minnie Mortar (1 medium round on M.4. emplacement (cricket) at N.30.c.5.3.5. and Mes work on Enemy Front line near this point. 20 medium rounds or more at 30.d.7.5.60 with excellent results. Considerable damage.	
RICHEBOURG	20		22 Medium rounds were fired on "CASTLE" enemy emplacement at M.30.c.52.32 two direct hits were obtained, but concrete position still remained. Six dropped 2 bombs of further down to road and small explosion heard. 1 medium round on N.26.a.50.10 in retaliation. 5 medium rounds on "FOX" at P.55.d.90.30. Considerable damage at 31.a.7.55 and 3 heavy rounds on "FOX" at P.55.d.90.30.	
AUBERS 36.S.W.1 Edition 8a 1/10,000	21		21 Heavy rounds on this at 525 y85.30. Were very much damaged. No Enemy T.M. activity.	
	22		4 Medium rounds were fired on N.16.b.30.75. Several high angle bombs fired from M.29.d.7.5. about 10 a.m.	
	23		There was no firing done today and no Enemy T.M. activity. Medium positions were inspected by the Corps Trench Mortar advisor.	
	24		Portuguese M.T. Mr attached to 4th group fired 4 rounds in retaliation to 3 enemy	

Army Form C. 2118.

WAR DIARY
or
INTELLIGENCE SUMMARY.
(Erase heading not required.)

May 1917   Sheet VII

49th Division Trench Mortar Batteries

Instructions regarding War Diaries and Intelligence Summaries are contained in F. S. Regs., Part II. and the Staff Manual respectively. Title pages will be prepared in manuscript.

Place	Date	Hour	Summary of Events and Information	Remarks and references to Appendices
LAVENTIE & RICHEBOURG 10 Maps RICHEBOURG 36 S.W.3 Edition 5a 1/10,000 1/10,000 AUBERS 36 S.W.1 Edition 5a 1/10,000	May 24th Cont'd 25 26 27		Vane bombs falling about M.29.b.70.95. 7/49 medium battery fired 25 rounds on enemy line at 5.20.d.90.30 with good results and 12 rounds on enemy T.M. at about B.10.a.86.30 in retaliation to 4 T.M.S. falling about 5.16.d.20.32. [initials]

2 medium rounds were fired on enemy front line in retaliation. About 12 Gratinewoofr fell near N ELGIN ST. between 7.25 a.m. and 8 a.m. Heavy and medium battery were employed in renovating position and resuming fire. [initials]

4/49 medium battery fired 28 rounds from M.18.d.95.16 on to enemy line at N.19.a.3.4. 4/49 fired 19 rounds on enemy wire and front line at M.35.a.97.50 2 medium rounds fired from M.35.a.60.90 but being aimed caused to burst in our own front line wounding one gunner of the gun, and burst in our own front line wounding one gunner gun. led had sunk rendering further firing from this position impossible Ordinary Medium battery attacked 9/49 fired 3 rounds on M.4 emplacement at M.36.a.5.3 and 31 rounds on 19.30.a.64, and M.30.a.6.3 in retaliation to Enemy Vane bombs falling in our line about 6 Gratinewoofr fell in our area in M.18.d. [initials]

7/49 Medium battery fired 62 rounds on the following points. Enemy wire at M.35.d.98.50., Enemy front line at M.35.a.92.45. and Enemy wire at M.35.a.81.42. with good results. A good deal of wire was blown up and destroy on enemy by L.T.M.S. Belgians M. battery attacked 9/49 fired 4 rounds on M.36.a.6.3 about 6 L.T.M.S. fell under enemy front line at M.35.a.66, M.35.a.60.65 also several Vane bombs fell in retaliation to our shelling from direction of M.36.a.55.10. [initials] | |

A.5834   Wt.W.4973/M687. 750,000. 8/16. D. D.& L. Ltd. Forms/C.2118/13.

Army Form C. 2118.

WAR DIARY
or
INTELLIGENCE SUMMARY.
(Erase heading not required.)

May 1917 Sheet VIII

49th Division Heavy Mortar Batteries

Place	Date	Hour	Summary of Events and Information	Remarks and references to Appendices
LAVENTIE & RICHEBOURG Nep Maps 36 SW 1 Edition 8d	May 28		25 medium rounds fired by X/49 on Enemy M.G. and Front Line at N.19.a.3.4 gave good results. Y/49 Medium battery fired 15 rounds on the wire at M35d.8.42. Portuguese battery attacked Y/49 fired 2 rounds on N.8.6 at M36a.9. Enemy T.M's fell on to CHATEAU REDOUBT and several L.T.M's on to Front Line between M35.a.6879 and M35d.55.60. Enemy shelled gun position at M35d.38.60 with 4.5.0. Several aerial torpedoes and L.T.M's fell about gun position at M35d top.	
RICHEBOURG 36 SW 1	29		10 Medium rounds were fired by X/49 battery in reprisal on the following points. Z/49 Medium battery fired 21 rounds on Track Houettes at S.16.b.60.60 and S.16.a.90.95, 3 rounds on S.10.d.60.50 in retaliation for hostile T.M. and 6 rounds on S.16.b.10.90. 3 rounds on M36.a.4.8 and 5 rounds on M30.a.9.9 in retaliation. A few Enemy Rifle grenades fell in our lines fired from N.13.c.9.3. and 6 Vane bombs also fell on our line near M30.a.6.W.	
AUBERS 36 SW 1 Edition 8d 1/10,000	30		4 Medium rounds were fired by X/49 battery on Enemy Front Line in retaliation. Z/49 Medium battery fired 33 rounds on the following points - 5 rounds on MITSI S.T. at S.10.d.60.50 in retaliation for hostile T.M. 15 rounds on TARAD TRENCH at S.10.d.90.00 and 6 MITSI TRENCH at S.11.c.10.20 and 4 rounds at S.16.b.00.85 in retaliation. Enemy Trench Tramway Truck blown up in X.19.c.5.3. Medium battery attacked Y/49 fired 11 rounds on M36.a.9.9 in retaliation. Heavy battery was called upon for retaliation over enemy T.M. Enemy observed mortars well.	

Army Form C. 2118.

WAR DIARY
or
INTELLIGENCE SUMMARY.

(Erase heading not required.)

May 1917 Sheet IX 49 L Division Trench Mortar Batteries

Place	Date	Hour	Summary of Events and Information	Remarks and references to Appendices
LAVENTIE & RICHEBOURG	May 30	(contd)	Sucked Hostile T.M.s fell on front line between M.35.a.68.98 and M.35.c.15.64 and 6 fell near support line north of PLUM ST. 6 bombs fell in our lines Fired M.35 & 64	
Ref Maps				
RICHEBOURG	31		2/1/9 Medium battery fired 17 rounds on M.17.51 O.T. in retaliation to Hostile T.M.s	
36 S.W.3			7 M.B. Section of trench tramway 1 clear of Portugues battery attached	
Sheet 8a			9/49 fired 26 rounds on M.36.a.7.8 and M.30.c.5.7 in retaliation	
1/10,000				
AUBERS				
36 S.W.1				
Edition 8a				
1/10,000				

SECRET.

WAR DIARY.

OF

Hqrs (nth) Div: Trench Mortar Batteries

FOR

June 1917.

Confidential

War Diary

of

119th Div: Trench Mortar Batteries

for

Month of June 1917.

Army Form C. 2118.

WAR DIARY
or
INTELLIGENCE SUMMARY

(Erase heading not required.)

49th Divisional Trench Mortar Batteries   June 1917   Sheet I

Instructions regarding War Diaries and Intelligence Summaries are contained in F. S. Regs., Part II. and the Staff Manual respectively. Title Pages will be prepared in manuscript.

Place	Date	Hour	Summary of Events and Information	Remarks and references to Appendices
LAVENTIE Ref Map 36 S.W.3 Edition 8a 1/10,000	June 1st		All 49th Division Trench Mortar Batteries are billeting in LAVENTIE. Divisional Trench Mortar Officer is also in LAVENTIE. The 2nd Portuguese T.M. Battery is attached to this Division for instructions. Y/49 Battery fired 21 rounds (mediums) on :- M.6. Emplacement at S.5.d.28.48 (retaliation) and Enemy wire at S.5.d.42.79. Portuguese Battery fired 24 rounds on Enemy wire. Several Enemy T.M's fell on to our front line between M.35.d.58.98 and M.35.d.68.88. Enemy shelled pill boxes at M.35.d.90.60 with 4.2's. The gun was flown over the parados and body & retention frame wrecked. Men of the Batteries have been twice trained in gas drill during the past week.	R.T.A.
RICHEBOURG AUBERS 36 S.W.1 Edition 8a 1/10,000	2nd		Z/49 Medium Battery retaliated to Hate T.M. with 5 rounds on S.22.c.80.40. Portuguese Battery fired 3 rounds on Enemy T.M. emplacement and 37 rounds in Enemy trenches and wire South of "Sugar Loaf". No enemy retaliation.	R.T.A.
	3rd		Heavy Battery fired 8 rounds on to S.5.d.50.30 in retaliation to Enemy T.M. which immediately ceased. Several Enemy L.T.M's fell on LA FONE ST.	R.T.A.
	4th		Z medium Battery fired 8 rounds on MITSI TRENCH at S.11.c.20.30. Heavy Bombardment of Enemy T.M's and Vane bombs on to LA FONE ST from 1-30 am to 2 am.	R.T.A.
	5th		Heavy mortar fired 13 rounds on S.5.b.42.24; M.36.c.23.10 and M.36.c.32.40 all were fired in retaliation. Several Enemy M.T.M's fired from the neighbourhood of BOIS du BIEZ fell on S.5.c.10.90 at 2 pm. A few L.T.M. fell on CHATEAU REDOUBT about 2.45 pm.	R.T.A.

Army Form C. 2118.

WAR DIARY
or
INTELLIGENCE SUMMARY

(Erase heading not required.)

June 1917 Sheet II

Aq Divisions Trench Mortar Batteries

Instructions regarding War Diaries and Intelligence Summaries are contained in F.S. Regs., Part II. and the Staff Manual respectively. Title Pages will be prepared in manuscript.

Place	Date June	Hour	Summary of Events and Information	Remarks and references to Appendices
LAVENTIE Ref maps 36 S.W.3 Edition 8a 1/10,000	6		X/ Medium Battery fired 6 registering rounds on N.14.a.82.40. Heavy Battery fired 13 on M.30.c.99.30; S.5.d.#2.24; S.5.c.25.92 & M.36.c.20.00 as covering fire for Medium Battery. Owing to difficulty on observation & erratic firing of the guns the shooting was poor.	MH
RICHEBOURG 36 S.W.3 Edition 8a 1/10,000	7		Medium Battery and at Ordnance Works to hope for repair. X/ Medium Battery fired 50 rounds at 11-0 pm on M.24.a.8.5, N.19.c.10.70 & N.19.c.95.50 in connection with a raid by the 146 Infantry Brigade the enemy retaliated with a few Van bombs. During the day Y/19 fired 105 rounds on the wire at the following points. S.5.b.75-65 & S.5.b.70.88; M.35.a.78.12 to M.35.d.98.24 much wire was destroyed especially at M.35.a.78.12. to which enemy retaliated with 4-25 from 11-0 am to 12.0 at 3 min intervals about M.35.a.4.9 (old position) Heavy Battery fired 20 rounds on M.30.d.80.60 & M.30.a.9560 Shooting was erratic owing to bad gun. One shot exploded 100 yards in front of gun. There was a marked absence of any serious retaliation. The huge not used with Heavy bombs is practically instantaneous and of no use against any strong position. The electric fuse if effective though - V/49.4.O.R. 110.O.R. X/49.1.O.R. 32.O.R. Y/49.3.O.R. 31.O.R. and Z/49.2.O.R. 33.O.R.	MH
AUBERS 36 S.W.1 Edition 8a 1/10,000	8		No firing has been done today. Enemy T.M.s very quiet.	MH
	9		Heavy Battery fired 22 rounds on M.36.c.25.15; M.35.a.85.40 & M.35.a.99.40 Owing to difficulties on observation & erratic firing of the guns the shooting was poor. X/ Battery fired 7 medium rounds on Enemy front line N.14.a.60.10. Enemy retaliated with whizz-bangs after 6" round. Men have been engaged in building new Up positions B.out stores et.	MH

Army Form C. 2118.

WAR DIARY or INTELLIGENCE SUMMARY

(Erase heading not required.)

49th Division Trench Mortar Batteries June 1917 Sheet III

Place	Date	Hour	Summary of Events and Information	Remarks and references to Appendices
LAVENTIE Reg Hqrs	June 10th		Heavy T3 artery fired 30 rounds on S.5.d.42.29, S.6.c.25.92, M.36.c.20.00 and M.36.c.22.10 in retaliation to Enemy T.M.'s. Enemy new on one T.M. position. There was considerable Enemy T.M. & Artillery Activity during the day. Work continued on new positions etc.	R.M.A
RUE BOUVRY 36 S.W.3 Eastern Ba. 10,000	11		A raid was carried out tonight by the 1/4 Y & L Regiment during which Y/49 artery fired 40 rounds, Y/49 Battery 28 and N/49 Heavy Battery 23 rounds Heavy Battery fired 20 rounds during the day in retaliation to Enemy T.M.'s throughout the raid Enemy retaliated with M.T.M.S, Rifle Bombs, Heavy Trench Mortars, 4.25 and 7.7 m.m Shells on our front line from FRITH C.T. to ELGIN C.T. Work has been done on our heavy position at MASSELOT Z/49 Medium Battery guns have been taken from MAUQUISSART Sector and put in FAUQUISSART Sector.	R.M.A
RUBERS 36 S.W.1 Eastern Ba. 10,000	12		Heavy Battery fired 30 rounds on S.6.c 25.92, M.36.c.20.00 and M.36.c.22.10 and M.29.c 93.10 in retaliation to enemy Heavy & Medium Mortars. 3 Direct hits on Gun pit made further firing impossible. Y/49 Medium artery fired 22 rounds on Enemy Trenches from 7-30 p.m until 1 a.m there was a general Enemy Bombardment such all types of T.M. between 1,000 & 1,500 rounds falling on front & reserve line from DUCKS BILL to OXFORD ST. During this bombardment the D.T.M. O (Capt R.I. Walker) and Lt & I Sheet (V/49 Battery) were gassed. Capt. R. H. Aldridge V/49 Battery is now acting D.T.M.O	R.M.A R.M.A
	13		No firing has been done today - Enemy Mortars very quiet.	
	14		No firing has been done today. Enemy Activity - Nil. Work has been continued on new positions and Bomb Stores. Staff of mortars to-day. 12 medium and 2 heavies. 3 medium mortars are out of action for repairs	R.M.A
	15		Effective Strong of Batteries. V/49. 3 Off. 107 O.R. X/49. 2 Off. 33. O.R. Y/49. 3 Off. 32. and Z/49. 2 Off. 33. O.R. No firing done today - Enemy Activity nil. Work on positions proceeding	R.M.A

Army Form C. 2118.

WAR DIARY
or
INTELLIGENCE SUMMARY

(Erase heading not required.)

June 1918 Sheet IV

49th Division Trench Mortar Batteries

Place	Date	Hour	Summary of Events and Information	Remarks and references to Appendices
LAVENTIE Rer.Map	June 16		34 medium rounds expended registering on Enemy front line & junction of C.T's. Work on new positions & bomb stores continued.	RWH
RICHEBOURG 36 NW 3	17		Z medium Battery fired 30 rounds on Enemy front line. X medium Battery fired 2 rounds on M.24.d.4510, N.19.a.3005, N.19.a.55.90. No Enemy retaliation.	RWH
Estaires 8a 1/10,000	18		35 medium rounds unwcutting on M.36.a.8030 & M.35.d.94.48 and 10 rounds unwcutting on S.6.b.41.90 and S.6.b.45.65. 62 medium rounds were fired on the following points with a view to harassing the Enemy M.24.d.45.10, N.19.c.15.80, N.19.a.45.85 and N.19.a.3005. Enemy retaliated with 10 "Pineapples" or or about N.8.0.33.	RWH
RUBERS 36 NW 1 Estaires 8a 1/10,000	19		Y medium Battery have expended 50 rounds unwcutting in connection with a proposed raid. A large gap was cut. Medium Batteris continued to harass the Enemy. 52 rounds being fired at intervals during the day on the following points. M.24.d.90.60, N.19.a.3000 & N.19.c.15.80. Enemy fired 20 pineapples on Reserve line from N.8.c.3.5. & N.13.a.2.5. A few pineapples on N.8.6.4 to unwcutting operations. 9 medium rounds fired on Enemy T.M. on S.5.c.80.43 & S.5.a.9.3 Men have been engaged carrying up bombs, materials etc and work on new positions and demolitions.	RWH
	20		Y medium Battery continued unwcutting 50 rounds being expended. Brigade medium Battery fired 49 rounds on Enemy front line & wire. 60 medium rounds were fired at intervals during the day on the Enemy front line. Enemy retaliated to unwcutting with 4-2's on NEW CUT ALLEY & about an hour Heavy Battery fired 12 rounds on the 9 emp. incidents at M.35.d.20.10 & M.36.c.00.50. Y medium Battery continued unwcutting 4 9's have now been cut for unwcutting. Portugese Battery expended 48 rounds unwcutting as a feint for unwcutting.	RWH
	21		by Y Battery. Harassing fire was continued today 48 rounds being fired at intervals. 22 rounds on m.35.d.60.30. Enemy retaliated with about 12 small Enemy Minnies on m.35.d.62.16 on September 1917 M.24.d.20.80 UGH on positions continued.	RWH

2449 Wt. W14957/M90 759,000 1/16 J.B.C. & A. Forms/C.2118/12.

Army Form C. 2118.

WAR DIARY or INTELLIGENCE SUMMARY.

(Erase heading not required.) 49th Divn. and Trench Mortar Batteries. June 1917 Sheet V

Instructions regarding War Diaries and Intelligence Summaries are contained in F.S. Regs., Part II. and the Staff Manual respectively. Title pages will be prepared in manuscript.

Place	Date	Hour	Summary of Events and Information	Remarks and references to Appendices
LAVENTIE Hq. Maps BICHEBOURG 36 d.W. 3 Fauton 8a 110,000 AUBERS 36.d.W.t. Fauton 8a 110,000	June 22		48 Medium Rounds on Enemy front line & work harassing fire. Slight Enemy T.M. activity between 12 and 2pm. Heavy Battery continued work on bomb dares & men have been twice trained in Gas Drill during the week.	MH
	23		Medium Batteries continued Harassing fire. The following rounds being expended. 18 on M.24.d.80.30, 19 on "THE LOZENGE", 35 on M.30.a.90.10, M.30.a.38.02, M.30.C.85.87. Much guns and timber were flown up at this later point. 10 rounds on M.14.a.90.30. Much timber was flown up, 42 rounds on Enemy front line between M.13.d.70.60 and M.8.d.35.15. Much damage was done. Heavy Battery fired 20 rounds on enemy T.M. positions at M.36.C.50.85 and M.36.C.50.10. Enemy T.M. Activity - Nil.	MH
	24		55 rounds Medium at intervals during the day on bounds:- M.8.d.40.10, M.14.d.45.80, M.14.a.90.20 and M.14.C.90.00, 50 rounds at irregular intervals on bounds M.30.a.80.02, M.30.C.80.90, M.30.C.65.40. And front line from M.30.a.40.10 to M.36.C.50.80. 40 rounds on Enemy front line from M.19.a.90.60 to M.19.d.60.30 and 62 rounds wirecutting on NEUVE CHAPELLE No.1. Heavy Battery fired 17 rounds on M.36.C.20.10 and T.M. Emplacement S.6.a.50.30 (Enemy returned to Battery wirecutting with 20. 7mm shells on position (S.5.a.85.37) a few hostile L.A.M. T.M. on our front line during the day. New temporary positions have been commenced for an intended T.M. bombardment.	MH
	25		19 rounds Heavy on Enemy T.M. M.36.C.20.00 and 40 Medium rounds harassing fire on Enemy front line and suspected T.M. Enemy retaliated with 6 salvoes of M.W. BIRDCAGE at 10.20 a.m. Work on new pits continued.	MH
	26		Heavy Battery fired 12 rounds in retaliation to Enemy T.M. & Lane Bombs. 53 Medium rounds on Enemy front line wire. Work on temporary positions continued.	MH
	27		Enemy - Nil - Enemy - Quiet. Work continued. Ammunition at 10cm up stock of Mortars. 12 Mediums. 4 Heavys.	MH
	28		Enemy - Nil - Enemy Activity - Nil. Effective rounds. 1/49. 3 9/, 105 O.R. 7/49. 2 8/. 51 O.R. and 2/49. 2 9/. 38 O.R.	MH

WAR DIARY
or
INTELLIGENCE SUMMARY.

Army Form C. 2118.

June 1917. Sheet VI
49th Division Trench Mortar Batteries

Place	Date	Hour	Summary of Events and Information	Remarks and references to Appendices
LAVENTIE Sh/maps 36cNW2	June 29		At 9.0 pm a trench mortar bombardment was commenced from the temporary positions built during the past few days. 16 Medium and 5 Heavy T.M. were used and 364 Medium & 104 Heavy rounds fired on Enemy front line between M.36.c.0.5 and S.5.d.45.00 and Road running through S.6.a. & 5 and S.5.d.) 2 direct hits was obtained on T.M. position at M.36.c.22.12. Artillery supported this bombardment with Gas shells & on Enemy Y.M. on machine gun emplacements. Enemy retaliation was practically nil. R.M.A. bombardment ceased at 9-30 pm. Portuguese L.Y. Mortar crew cleared firing 3,410 rounds R.M.A. Firing - nil. About 6 Enemy R.T.M.s fell on CHATEAU REDOUBT about dusk day	
RICHEBOURG 36NW3 Edition 8a. 1/10,000				
AUBERS 36NW1 Edition 8a. 1/10,000	30		Ammunition Expended during June. Medium 1942. Heavy 522. Casualties during June. Killed nil. Wounded 2 Officers (Gas) 2 O.R. (Gas) 1 O.R. (S.W.)	

R.H. Newitt (?) Capt. Comdg.
49th (W.R.) T.M. Bryd.

11 Confidential Vol 8

War Diary

of

119th vis French Mortars

for

Month of July 1917

Army Form C. 2118.

WAR DIARY
or
INTELLIGENCE SUMMARY
(Erase heading not required.)

Sheet I
July 1919
H.Q. "Division Trench Mortar Batteries

Instructions regarding War Diaries and Intelligence Summaries are contained in F. S. Regs., Part II. and the Staff Manual respectively. Title Pages will be prepared in manuscript.

Place	Date	Hour	Summary of Events and Information	Remarks and references to Appendices
LAVENTIE REF MAPS RICHEBOURG 36 S.W. 3 Eastings 1/10,000 AUBERS 36 S.W. 1 Eastings 1/10,000	July 1.		All Batteries billeted in LAVENTIE with detachments in the line. V/49 Heavy Battery fired 1 round registration. Enemy activity - Nil.	V/49
	2		H Heavy rounds on enemy T.M. at M.36.c.22.10. Enemy ceased fire. Battery fired 35 rounds at items on Enemy front line from 3.5.6.63.30 to 3.5.k.70.90 During operations by Portuguese Division. Y/49 Medium Battery fired 3 rounds retaliation on GRETCHEN TRENCH at M.36.a.55.85. Retaliation. 6 Grenatenwerfen fell on 70.13.a.95.05 and a few 7.6 Y.M. fell in the vicinity of front line near SUNKEN ROAD and 2.W.Y.M. and a 2.M. Y.M. on front line in front of Neuve Chapelle	V/49 Y/49
	3		10 Heavy rounds (registration) on N.25.a.63.98 and N.14.d.35.15. During night raid 75 Medium rounds fired on GRETCHEN TRENCH. Between 1 & 2 a.m. Enemy bombarded front line, C.T.s, and support line with light, medium & Heavy T.M.s and shelled with NEUVE CHAPELLE and DEAD HORSE COPSE with 4.2's and 77mm. The latter gun was particularly heavily shelled during the whole period. 1. 4.2 within 3ft. of the gun and 77mm Shrapnel just live to the Camouflage and sandbags round the Mount. Also moving strong unobservable Medium Battery Catalogue no retaliation to this, owing to our Infantry patrol and wiring party being in "No man's land"	V/49 Y/49
	4		2 6" Mortar and 36 6" M.R. are held in readiness to proceed to 101 Army School of Mortar for instruction on 6" Newton Trench Mortars. Y/49 2" M. Battery fired 3 rounds retaliation on GRETCHEN TRENCH a few rounds M.T.M. fell in the vicinity of SUNKEN ROAD. Slack of Mortars today is V/49. 4 Heavy 9.45" x H.9. 4 Medium 2". Y/49 4 Medium 2" and 2/49. 4 Medium 2". Casualties 1 man slightly wounded.	V/49 Y/49

2449 Wt. W14957/M90 750,000 1/16 J.B.C. & A. Forms/C.2118/12.

Army Form C. 2118.

WAR DIARY
or
INTELLIGENCE SUMMARY

(Erase heading not required.) H.Q. 2 Division Trench Mortar Batteries July 1917 Sheet II

Instructions regarding War Diaries and Intelligence Summaries are contained in F. S. Regs., Part II. and the Staff Manual respectively. Title Pages will be prepared in manuscript.

Place	Date	Hour	Summary of Events and Information	Remarks and references to Appendices
LAVENTIE REF: MAP: RICHEBOURG 36.N.W.3 Edition 8a 1/10,000	5		Y/49 Heavy Battery fired 13 rounds with good results on front line from N.8.a. 50.20 to N.8.a. 30.86. Earth boards are being thrown up. 6 medium rounds were fired on N.19.c.05.70 and DORA C.T. at N.9.c.15.25 at the request of the Infantry. Portugese Medium Battery fired 31 rounds retaliation on Enemy front line. Several shells on X/M's fell on S.6.a.95.40 and S.6.a.85.90 enemy retaliated to Heavy Battery fire with lashing barrage which fell near our line did no damage.	R.M.A
			Electric Strength of Batteries to-day Y/49 3 Off. 104 O.R. X/49 3 Off. 31. O.R. Y/49. 3 Off. 31. O.R. and Z/49 3 Off. 32. O.R.	R.M.A
AUBERS 36.N.W.1 Edition 8a 1/10,000	6		Z/49 Medium Battery fired 45 rounds on Enemy strong point N.8.a.30.05. at request of Left Group R.O. Effect of fire good, much damage done. Portug: also Medium Battery fired 82 rounds on Enemy front line in retaliation for Enemy T.M. on S.5.a.80.50 and S.5.a.85.26	R.M.A
	7		Parts to failed proceeded to 1st Army school for instruction on 6" newton T.M. 5 Medium rounds at request of Infantry on N.19.a.35.28. 25" Medium rounds on Enemy front line N.14.a.90.58 and N.14.a.53.00. Portuguese Battery fired 30 rounds on L.5.c.75.70. Heavy Battery fired 1 round registration shot 13 rounds on M.G. Emplacement near IRMA TRENCH. Good results were obtained. Enemy fired 30 rounds in or about 50 yards of aug out was blown in. Bat-trench Coln no 2 was ruined and Coln no 2 damaged	R.M.A
	8		Portuguese Medium Battery fired 4 rounds on S.5. X.72.85 with good effect. The relief of the H.Q. 2 Division Trench Mortar Batteries was commenced by Portuguese Division.	R.M.A
	9		Relief of H.Q. 2 Division Trench Mortar Batteries completed at 6 p.m. Y/63 Y.M. Batteries relieved Y/49. Portuguese Division Y.M. Batteries relieved medium mortars	R.M.A

2449 Wt. W14957/M90 750,000 1/16 J.B.C. & A. Forms/C.2118/12.

Army Form C. 2118.

WAR DIARY
or
INTELLIGENCE SUMMARY

Sheet II. July 1917
49th Division Trench Mortar Batteries

(Erase heading not required.)

Place	Date	Hour	Summary of Events and Information	Remarks and references to Appendices
LE SART.	July 10.		49th Division T.M. Batteries marched to LE SART (map ref. K.27.c.). Medium Mortars were taken. Heavy Mortars were all handed over on the line, together with their map plans etc.	RMA
Ry. Map: FRANCE Sheet 36 a Edition 6	11		Batteries resting at LE SART.	RMA
	12		Batteries resting at LE SART.	RMA
	13		Removal of Medium Batteries on charts for instructors on 6" Newton T.M. commenced today.	RMA
LEFFRINGHOUCKE Ref. map: BELGIUM & FRANCE SHEET 19 (Edition 2)	14		Batteries marched to LESTREM and entrained, arrived and detrained at DUNKERQUE and marched to LEFFRINGHOUCKE. (map ref. I.4.c.10.15).	RMA
	15		Batteries were marching etc.	RMA
TETEGHEM map ref.: I.15 a. 80.00 Ry.Map: BELGIUM & FRANCE SHEET 19	16		Moved to billets in TETEGHEM. Capt Walker & 8th/4th shell rejoined from Base.	RMA
	17		Batteries were marching etc.	RMA
	18		Heavy Battery moved to COXYDE (map ref X.13. b. 80.60) Medium Batteries still at TETEGHEM.	RMA
COXYDE Ry.Map: OOST-DUNKERKE SHEET 11.	19		Heavy Battery came over 32nd Division Heavy Battery at NIEUPORT and COXYDE.	RMA
	20.		Heavy Battery working under D.T.M.O 32nd Division. Medium Batteries at TETEGHEM.	RMA
	21		Medium Batteries arrived at COXYDE. D.T.M.O. billeted at COXYDE-LES-BAINS.	
	22		Medium Batteries are engaged in practice for 6" Newton T.M. and heavy Batteries on Heavy Battery practice. 2 officers have been lent by B.R.G. Battery on this unit. 2/49 Battery remained in NIEUPORT 42 men by 1/49 T.M. Battery were taken to reinforce suffering from Gas effects caused by German Gas Shell bombardment of NIEUPORT during the night 21/22	RMA

Army Form C. 2118.

WAR DIARY
or
INTELLIGENCE SUMMARY

(Erase heading not required.)

July 1917 Sheet IV

Hq. Division French Mortar Batteries

Instructions regarding War Diaries and Intelligence Summaries are contained in F.S. Regs., Part II. and the Staff Manual respectively. Title Pages will be prepared in manuscript.

Place	Date	Hour	Summary of Events and Information	Remarks and references to Appendices
COXYDE. Ref. Map. BELGIUM Sheet 11 NIEUPORT Ref. Map. NIEUPORT 12. S.W.1 Section 2a.	July 23.		Heavy Battery fired 10 rounds in each of the following points in reply to S.E.S. - M.16.a. 45.30. M.17.c.15.82. M.23.a.80.65. & M.23.b.92.90. and 10 rounds in Charlie O.P. at M.17.c.01.20. Y/49 Y.M. Battery are engaged in Artillery Tract. X & Z Batteries are returning each shot at NIEUPORT and are working on 6" newton positions taking up guns and stocking ammunition. Carrying party of 200 infantry gave assistance with ammunition carrying today.	RMTA
	24		Heavy Battery fired 30 rounds onto trench M.24 Central & M.24.a.00.90 and 10 rounds at O.P.s at M.17.c.00.20. Several direct hits were obtained on Trench target. Cement Paint and other material for 6" positions taken up 1.0/ and 30 men of the 2nd Division reported to O.C. Y/49 at NIEUPORT to assist with work. The following T.M's are in charge. 9. 4.5" long. 8. 240.m.m. trench long 3. 6" trench Mortar (newton) (not yet in action) 6. Medium 2" (empirical to put into action 16.)	RMTA
	25		Heavy Battery fired 10 rounds in trench at M.24.a.50.40. Observations were difficult owing to mist. During the night the tunnel of no.5 emitter blown in. Closed the trench because breathing. Good progress made with Artillery tracks. Ammunition taken up to positions. Work on 6" positions etc.	RMTA
	26		6" heavy mounds fired in trenches against M.18.c.30.10. Other firing impossible owing to mist. Ammunition and material taken up. Work on Artillery tract and ventilation continued. 4 newton 6" T.M's received from DADOS.	RMTA
	27		500 rounds 6" newton ammunition taken up. Infantry party of 200 gave assistance. 15 Heavy rounds on enemy trenches and cross roads at M.16.5. & 96.18. One second shot BAYNE ISLANDS. 15" heavy rounds on BAM BOROUGH WALK.	RMTA

2449 Wt. W14957/M90 750,000 1/16 J.B.C. & A. Forms/C.2118/12.

WAR DIARY
or
INTELLIGENCE SUMMARY July 1917 Sheet V

(Erase heading not required.)

Army Form C. 2118.

49th Division Trench Mortar Batteries

Place	Date	Hour	Summary of Events and Information	Remarks and references to Appendices
COXYDE Ref Map BELGIUM Sheet 11	July 28		Further 6" Ammunition was taken up by G.S. Wagon to NIEUPORT a carrying party of 200 Infantry assisting. Medium battalio with carrying from NIEUPORT to Gun Position & Heavy ammunition on O.P. at M.14.c.00.20. Shooting very erratic 3 rounds short 3 rounds registration on GREY GABLES at M.18.c.30.10. 9 rounds on Enemy Trench at M.24.a.30.62. The last round went off prematurely while being laid & therefore shoot was very good. Infantry carrying party mentioned above failed to report.	R/VII
NIEUPORT Ref Map NIEUPORT 1:10,000 Edt 2.A.	29		A further 500 Newton 6" Ammunition taken up. Numerous Aerial Photos are being received showing condition of Enemy Line from time to time. 39 Heavy rounds were fired on BAMBURGH WALK from M.24 central to M.24.a.00.86. 63 Heavy rounds were fired on BAMBURGH WALK from M.24 central & M.24.a.00.86. Work on all positions is being proceeded with. Results were good.	R/VII
	30		39 medium Heavy on BAMBURGH WALK M.24 central to M.24.a.00.86. Two rounds were premature. The damaging no H pit, the other severely damaging no 3 pit and passage to pit and entirely destroying gun. Work on positions for 6 Newtons continued.	R/VII
	31		Battery strength today as follows:- 4/49. 57. O.R. 4/49. 30. O.R. 4/49. 32. O.R. 7/49. 32. O.R. Medium & Heavy were fired today on GROOTE BAMBURGH FARM and BAMBURGH WALK at M.24 central. Range tables for 6" Newton T.M. with supercharge were received from 2nd Army School of Mortars. Ammunition Expended Medium 2" = 288 Heavy 9.45 = 421 Casualties Wounded 4 Gassed etc 55 Accidental 3 Injuries 62	

R.H.Fairlie
Capt. Comdg.
49th (W.R.) T.M. Btys.

Confidential

War Diary

of the 9th Battalion

for the

month of August 1917

Vol 9

Original

Army Form C. 2118.

WAR DIARY or INTELLIGENCE SUMMARY

(Erase heading not required.)

August 1914   Sheet 1

49th Division French Mortar Batteries

Place	Date	Hour	Summary of Events and Information	Remarks and references to Appendices
COXYDE REF: MAP BELGIUM Sheet 11 NIEUPORT REF: MAP NIEUPORT 13 S.W. 1 Edn. 2A	Aug 1st		Batteries are still Billeted in COXYDE VILLE. V/49 Battery have detachments in NIEUPORT. Z/49 are engaged clearing 6" Mortar T.M. Ammunition in NIEUPORT. D.3.M.O. Aid station furnished an advance report on 110 fuze used with 9.45" V/49 T.M.B. received 19 Ammunition. Heavy Battery fired 52 rounds on Lorry TRENCH between M.23.d.70.52. M.26.23.a.65.70. An explosion was caused at M.23.a.97.72	
	2		Heavy Battery fired 50 rounds on BAMBURGH TRENCH & GROOTE BAMBURGH FARM & R very good effect 6" Mortar Ammunition taken up.	
	3		32nd 49 Division T.M.B. Batteries relieved 49 Division T.M.B. Batteries at COXYDE VILLE. Freds and Communication with the exception of 2" L.M.B. out of action at COXYDE VILLE. Freds and ammunition from S. & 6 gun Ammunition carrying have been performed.	
	4 to 7		Batteries resting at COXYDE. Gas Drills, marching Drills etc. were carried out.	
	8			
	9		9 Reinforcements were received today from I.B.B. for Z/49 T.M.B.	
	10		A brief martial was held at COXYDE. On No.76/27 Battery Orr to Lieut. K. Ivan.	
	11		Batteries were inspected by the G.O.C. R.A. 49 Division at COXYDE Bains. Effective strength of the Batteries at present :- V/49. 5 Off. 67. O.R. Y/49 H. 4 Off. 30 or X/49. 3 Off. 32. O.Rs. Z/49 H. 4 Off 30 or Z/49. 3 Off 32. ORs. V/49 Heavy 3 detachments in the line under 3? or 2 M.O	
	12		Programme of Drill etc carried out.	
	13		do	
	14		do	
	15		Working parties of 1 Off and 12 O.R. engaged on Dug-outs for O.R. & S.R. remainder continued Drill, lectures etc.	

Army Form C. 2118.

WAR DIARY
or
INTELLIGENCE SUMMARY

(Erase heading not required.) August 1917 Sheet II 49th Division Trench Mortar Batteries

Instructions regarding War Diaries and Intelligence Summaries are contained in F.S. Regs., Part II and the Staff Manual respectively. Title Pages will be prepared in manuscript.

Place	Date	Hour	Summary of Events and Information	Remarks and references to Appendices
COXYDE Ry. Map BELGIUM Sheet II NIEUPORT 12. S.W.1 Edn 2.A	Aug 16		Two Officers and 3 O.R. proceeded to 4th Army school of T. Mortars for course of instruction on 6" Newton T.M. Detachments of V/49 Battery relieved the line were relieved by V/32 & No. 13. T.M. at Craywic. engaged on Drills etc.	
	17 to 23		Batteries are providing working parties for R.G.A. and V/49 Battery men are being sent to the Farm for 3 days rest at XV Corps Rest Station. Remained in morning at COXYDE engaged on Physical Drill, Gas Drill, Gun Drill etc.	
	24		Effective Strength of Batteries to-day V/49 V.M.B. 4 H.M. 69, O.R. V/49 H.M. 4 30 O.R. Z/49. 3 O. 29.O.R. Capt R.J. Waller. has now taken over the duties of D.T.M.O. Vice Capt. B.M. Alexander who handed command of V/49 to Lieut P. [?]	
	25		Firing of Mortars today. 30 medium 2" and 20 antibills. Batteries are still providing working parties to R.G.A.	
	26 to 31		Batteries are still out of action and are billeted in COXYDE with the exception of personnel engaged by wire to Field Batteries. Personnel at COXYDE engaged in Drills, Route Marches. etc & sports	
			Casualties during the month. Ammunition Expended	
			1 Off. 13 O.R. wounded (gas) 52 rounds 9·45" 1 O.R. accidental injuries	

Lewalker .... Capt. Comdg.
49th T.M. Bdys.

Confidential

No 10

17 49th Division

Trench Mortar Batteries

War Diary

September 1917

Army Form C. 2118.

WAR DIARY
or
INTELLIGENCE SUMMARY

49th DIVISION TRENCH MORTAR BATTERIES.

(Erase heading not required.) SEPTEMBER 1917 - Sheet 1.

Instructions regarding War Diaries and Intelligence Summaries are contained in F.S. Regs., Part II. and the Staff Manual respectively. Title Pages will be prepared in manuscript.

Reference Map:- North West Europe Sheet 1 and part of 4 - 1/250,000

Place	Date	Hour	Summary of Events and Information	Remarks and references to Appendices
Coxyde	1st to 7th		Batteries in Billets in COXYDE (Square B.6.) - No detachments in the line - Personnel instructed in Gas Drill, Gun Drill, Marching Drill, Physical Drill etc.	
	8th		80 N.C.O's and men of the Batteries were taken by Lorries to the 30th Division Area. (Square D.9.-) to work on positions for 49th Division Field Batteries. Remainder of personnel and stores moved by Lorry to UXEM (Square B.6.)	
Uxem	9th		Resting at UXEM	
Wormhoult	10th		Moved by Lorry to WORMHOULT (Square A.8.)	
	11th		Stores and personnel left with Batteries moved to CROIX DE POPERINGHE (West of DRANOUTRE) (Square C.9.) and are now under the orders of the 30th Division Artillery. D.T.M.O. Billetted at STRAZEELE (Square C.9.) with 49th Division Artillery Headquarters.	
CROIX DE POPERINGHE DRANOUTRE	12th to 27th		Personnel engaged on work for the 49th Division Field Batteries.	
WATOU	28th		Personnel of Trench Mortar Batteries who have been attached to Field Batteries returned and Batteries proceeded by road to WATOU (Square B.8.)	
	29th 30th		80 N.C.O's and men again attached to Field Batteries and taken up by Lorry to the New Area (D.8.) Remainder of Personnel still billetted at WATOU.	

D.T.M.O. Captain R.F.A.
49th (W.R.) Division.

CONFIDENTIAL Vol 11

War Diary

of

49th Bn French Border Battery

for

Month of October 1917

Army Form C. 2118.

WAR DIARY
or
INTELLIGENCE SUMMARY

49th (W.R.) Divisional Trench Mortar Batteries, R.A.

OCTOBER 1917.

(Erase heading not required.)

Instructions regarding War Diaries and Intelligence Summaries are contained in F. S. Regs., Part II. and the Staff Manual respectively. Title Pages will be prepared in manuscript. Reference maps Sheet 27 & 28 1/40,000.

Place	Date	Hour	Summary of Events and Information	Remarks and references to Appendices
WATOU. and near GRAVENSTAFEL	OCT 1st to 31st		No Trench Mortars have been in action during month owing to the Divisional Artillery being engaged in offensive operations in front of PASSCHENDAELE. The Trench Mortar personnel have been employed with the Field Batteries the whole of the month as working parties near GRAVENSTAFEL (in the vicinity of C.18.d.) About 20 men were kept at WATOU to relieve men for baths etc. 30 men have been given leave to the United Kingdom during the month. Strength of the Batteries to-day 10 Officers and 126 O.R's. Casualties. Wounded:- 5 Other Ranks. Ammunition expended NIL	

Walker Captain R.F.A.
Commanding, 49th (W.R.) Divisional Trench Mortar Batteries R.A.

17   Vol 12

Confidential
War Diary
4ᵗʰ Division Trench mortar
Batteries.
November 1917

Army Form C. 2118.

WAR DIARY
or
INTELLIGENCE SUMMARY.
(Erase heading not required.)

Instructions regarding War Diaries and Intelligence Summaries are contained in F. S. Regs., Part II. and the Staff Manual respectively. Title pages will be prepared in manuscript.

Place	Date	Hour	Summary of Events and Information	Remarks and references to Appendices
			Reference maps. Sheet 27 & 28 BELGIUM 1/40,000.	
WATOU. YPRES.	Nov, 1st to 30th.		49th DIVISION TRENCH MORTAR BATTERIES.	
			NO Trench Mortars have been in action during the month.	
			Personnel has been employed with the 49th Division Field Batteries as working parties at	
			the Battery positions near GRAVENSTAVEL. Rest billets at WATOU.	
			Effective strength of the Batteries to date. Officers 10. Other ranks 121.	
	28th.		Lieut. J.L.SOWINSKI M.C. killed in action by enemy shell & buried on 29th in cemetary at VLAMERTINGHE.	
			Casualties.	
			Ammunition expended. Officers Other ranks.	
			NIL Killed 1 Killed 1 Wounded 1.	
			P.J.Walker Captain R.F.A.	
			Commanding, 49th Division Trench Mortar Batteries, P.M.A.	

14 Confidential
War Diary
49 Inf. Trench Mortar Battery
for the month of December
1917

VII 13

Army Form C. 2118

WAR DIARY
or
INTELLIGENCE SUMMARY

(Erase heading not required.)

Instructions regarding War Diaries and Intelligence Summaries are contained in F. S. Regs., Part II. and the Staff Manual respectively. Title Pages will be prepared in manuscript.

Place	Date	Hour	Summary of Events and Information	Remarks and references to Appendices
			49th DIVISIONAL TRENCH MORTAR BATTERIES.	
YPRES.	Dec. 1st 2nd.		Personnel of Batteries engaged on fatigues for the Field Artillery Batteries.	
VIEUX BERQUIN.	3rd.		Moved with the 49th Divisional Artillery to the BERQUIN (rest) area.	
	4th to 31st.		Programme of Training carried out as per appendix.	
	20th		Z Battery proceeded to the Fourth Army Trench Mortar school at VAUX-EN-AMIENOIS for Training in 6" Newton Trench Mortar Drill.	

Captain. R.F.A.

Commanding, 49th Division Trench Mortar Batteries.

1875 Wt. W.593/826 1,000,000 4/15 J.B.C. & A. A.D.S.S./Forms/C. 2118.

49th Div¹ T.M. Battery. Programme of Training for week ending 30.12.17
VIEUX BERQUIN

TIME	MONDAY	TUESDAY	WEDNESDAY	THURSDAY	FRIDAY	SATURDAY	SUNDAY
	Working parties to		Artillery Brigade		Average number of men 20		Church Parade
9.30am to 12.50	Remainder Physical Drill. Revolver Practice Machine Drill	Squad Drill Signalling	Gas Helmet Drill Stretchers Drill Revolver Practice Squad Drill	Physical Drill Signalling	Physical Drill Revolver Practice Kit Inspection	Physical Drill Drill Inspection Scout Billets	C.O's Inspection of Billets

Afternoon Recreational Training throughout the week.

S/Lt Hobson a/c Capt R.F.A.
Comdg Vieux B. T.M. Battery.

Vol 14

Confidential

War Diary

of M.O. 49 for

month of January 1915

Army Form C. 2118.

WAR DIARY
or
INTELLIGENCE SUMMARY.
(Erase heading not required.)

Instructions regarding War Diaries and Intelligence Summaries are contained in F. S. Regs., Part II. and the Staff Manual respectively. Title pages will be prepared in manuscript.

Place	Date	Hour	Summary of Events and Information	Remarks and references to Appendices
VIEUX BERQUIN	Jan: 1st. to 4th.		All Batteries carried out Marching Drill, Physical Drill, Rifle Drill Gas Drill Saluting Drill. Reference Map HAZEBROUCK 5A. 1/100,000.	
do	4th.		Moved from VIEUX BERQUIN to NOORDPEENE.	
NOORDPEENE	5th to 31st		All Batteries. - Mornings - Physical Drill, Marching Drill Rifle Drill Signalling etc. Afternoons - Organised Recreational Training.	
			Courses. - Lieut. R.C. OLDFIELD and 4 Other Ranks attended course which assembled at LEULINGHAM on 6th Jan: Course lasted 14 days.	
			Lieut. G.E. WEAR and 10 O.Rs. attended course which assembled at LEULINGHAM on 20th January. Course lasted 14 days.	
			Lieut. G.L. SHIEL M.C., 2/Lieut. A.L. FINDING and 22 Other Ranks attended 6" Newton T.M. Course which assembled at VAUX-EN-AMIENOIS (Near AMIENS) which assembled on 20th January. Duration of course 14 days.	

R.J.Walker . Captain,

D.T.M.O. 49th (W.R.) Division.

Vol 15

Confidential
War Diary

1st Div: Trench Mortar Batteries

February 1918.

Army Form C. 2118.

WAR DIARY
or
INTELLIGENCE SUMMARY

49th (W.R.) Division Trench Mortar Batteries.

(Erase heading not required.) February 1918.

Ref. Maps:- Hazebrouck 5 A 1/100,000 Sheet 28 1/40,000

Place	Date	Hour	Summary of Events and Information	Remarks and references to Appendices
NOORDPEENE	Feb. 1st		49th Division Trench Mortar Batteries in G.H.Q. Reserve with 49th Divisional Artillery at NOORDPEENE.	
	2nd.		do do do	
	3rd.		15 O.R. proceeded on Newton 6" Trench Mortar course at Fourth Army School.	
	4th to 9th		Instructions received to reorganize Trench Mortar Batteries under Authority of G.H.Q. O.B./166 dated 20/1/18. R.G.A. personnel serving with 49th Div. T.M.Batteries were transferred to Xth and XXIInd Corps to form Corps Heavy Trench Mortar Batteries. No Heavy Trench Mortar Batteries on now on the strength of a Division. The D.T.M.O. has therefore under his Command two newly formed Medium 6" Newton Trench Mortar Batteries (X/49 and Y/49) made up entirely of R.H. and R.F.A. personnel. Establishment of Medium Battery:- 4 Officer and 52 O.R.	
	10th to 21st		Batteries engaged Drilling, Recreational Training and Fatigues.	
KRUISTRAAT	22nd		Batteries moved by Lorry from NOORDPEENE to KRUISTRAAT (H.27.b.7.7.) where they billet for the night.	
GHELUVELT SECTOR.	23rd		49th Division Trench Mortar Batteries relieved the New Zealand Division Trench Mortar Batteries in the line in the GHELUVELT sector. 12 6" Newton T.Ms taken over, 8 of which are in action, positions for the remaining 4 being incomplete. Relief complete by 4-0 p.m. Headquarters X/49 T.M.B. CAMBRIDGE HOUSE (I.11.d.5.5.): Headquarters Y/49 T.M.B. I.16.c.5.7. D.T.M.O. with 49th Divisional Artillery H.Q. RAMPARTS YPRES (I.14.b.1.8.)	
	24th		10 rounds fired. Work on New positions, Ammunition fatigues etc.	
	25th		10 rounds fired.	do
	26th		Firing Nil.	do
	27th		do	do
	28th		do	do

MWalker Captain. R.F.A.

D.T.M.O. 49th (W.R.) Division,

21 / VX16

Confidential.

War Diary

19th Trench Mortar Batteries.

March 1918.

Army Form C. 2118.

WAR DIARY
or
INTELLIGENCE SUMMARY
(Erase heading not required.)

Instructions regarding War Diaries and Intelligence Summaries are contained in F.S. Regs., Part II. and the Staff Manual respectively. Title Pages will be prepared in manuscript.

Place	Date	Hour	Summary of Events and Information	Remarks and references to Appendices
GELUVELT SECTOR.	March 1st.		49th Divisional Trench Mortar Batteries. R.A. Ref: Map: BELGIUM Sheet 28 N.E. 1/20,000. MARCH 1918. 49th Divisional Trench Mortar Batteries have 10 Medium 6" Trench Mortars in action and two out of action for which positions are being made. Positions and S.O.S. points as follows:- X/49 T.M.B. No.1. J.10.b.6.3. S.O.S.Point. J.17.c.20.75. X/49 T.M.B. No.2. J.10.b.6.4. S.O.S.Point. J.17.c.20.75. X/49 T.M.B. No.3. J.10.b.6.5. S.O.S. point J.11.d.61.08. X/49 T.M.B. No.4. J.10.b.63.55. S.O.S.Point. J.17.b.02.68. X/49 T.M.B. No.5. J.10.b.95.60. S.O.S.Point, J.11.d.83.21. X/49 T.M.B. No.6. J.10.b.95.55. S.O.S.Point. J.12.c.64.81. Y/49 T.M.B. No.1. J.11.a.25.30. S.O.S.Point. J.12.a.92.85. Y/49 T.M.B. No.2&, J.11.a.25.35. S.O.S.Point. J.6.c.90.02. Y/49 T.M.B. No.3. J.4.d.83.90. S.O.S.Point. J.6.a.55.35. Y/49 T.M.B. No.4. J.4.b.90.16. S.O.S.Point. J.6.a.55.50. Y/49 T.M.B. Bo.5. D.22.d.70.05. S.O.S.Point. D.24.c.33.58. Y/49 T.M.B. No.6. D.28.b.70.95. S.O.S.Point. D.24.c.40.58.	
	2nd.		Situation quiet Ammunition carried up and work on positions for two Mortars proceeded with.	

signature Captain.R.F.A.
for. D.T.M.O. 49th (W.R.) Division.

2449 Wt. W14957/M90 750,000 1/16 J.B.C. & A. Forms/C.2118/12.

Army Form C. 2118.

WAR DIARY
or
INTELLIGENCE SUMMARY

Page 2.

(Erase heading not required.)

Instructions regarding War Diaries and Intelligence Summaries are contained in F. S. Regs., Part II. and the Staff Manual respectively. Title Pages will be prepared in manuscript.

Place	Date	Hour	Summary of Events and Information	Remarks and references to Appendices
GELUVELT SECTOR.	March 3rd.		Situation quiet. Ammunition on hand X/49 T.M.B. 327 rounds Y/49 T.M.B. 310.	
	4th.		Everything reported quiet - work on positions proceeded with.	
	5th.		Assisted by a carrying party of 30 men from the Infantry 100 rounds Ammunition carried up from the Dump to the Guns. Very slight enemy activity.	
	6th.		Slight hostile activity on tracks near positions between 10 a.m. and 12 noon. Intense bombardment at 7-30 p.m. on Front trenches and round T.M. positions duration 5 - 10 minutes.	
	7th		Everything reported very quiet - normal work on positions, detachments on Mortars etc.	
	8th.		Slight Hostile activity during the day near Y/49 T.M.B. positions.	
	9th.		X/49 T.M.B. fired 62 rounds in a Hurricane bombardment of enemy positions in Cemetery and Pill box in J.11.d. with good effect.	
	10th.		Very heavy Hostile shelling round position J.11.a.4.4. Machine gun fire and intermittent shelling during the night. Much aerial activity. No damage was done to T.M. positions. Position at D.24.c.33.58. was heavily shelled for One hour and 25 mins commencing 2-30 p.m. small communication trench between the two dug-outs hit and smashed in. Position again shelled during the night from 11 p.m. to 4 a.m. (124 shells) Machine guns very active. Other Sectors quiet.	
	11th.		Situation reported quiet- Intermittent shelling with gas shell just in rear of T.M. positions. X/49 T.M.B. fired 8 rounds.	
	12th.		Ammunition carried up and work on positions proceeded with. Enemy activity normal.	

R.H.Denure

Captain. R.F.A.

for D.T.M.O. 49th (W.R.) Division.

Army Form C. 2118.

WAR DIARY
or
INTELLIGENCE SUMMARY

(Erase heading not required.)

Page 3.

Instructions regarding War Diaries and Intelligence Summaries are contained in F. S. Regs., Part II. and the Staff Manual respectively. Title Pages will be prepared in manuscript.

Place	Date	Hour	Summary of Events and Information	Remarks and references to Appendices
GELUVELT SECTOR.	13th.		82 rounds fired by X/49 T.M.B. on targets in J.11.d. in Support of a raid. Situation reported very quiet. Normal work on positions etc.	
	14th.		One other rank killed, 2Lt. C.G.SCOTT and 1 O.R. wounded on position at J.11.a.25.30. by splinters from enemy shell. Position was continuously shelled during daylight. No damage done to position. Considerable shelling of ridge behind position between 6 and 7 p.m..	
	15th.		Intermittent shelling during the night near Y/49 T.M.B. positions, otherwise very quiet. Normal work on guns and positions proceeded with.	
	16th.		Right sector quiet during the morning - Support trenches in rear of positions shelled between 3-30 and 4 p.m. Ammunition carried up and normal work continued.	
	17th.		Position at J.4.d.85.90. shelled between 10-30 and 11 p.m. and again more heavily between 2-30 and 5-30 a.m. - No damage reported - Other positions quiet.	
	18th.		Normal Activity of Hostile Artillery round positions.	
	19th.		Positions at J.11.a.25.30. and J.11.d.25.25. heavily shelled at 6-30 a.m. for about 10 mins Positions at J.4.d.83.90. and J.4.b.90.16. were also heavily shelled passage from Bomb Store to gun pit smashed in.	
	21st.		Brisk shelling round positions in J.11.a.25.35. one large shell bursting at the entrance to the tunnel. X/49 T.M.B. Fired 42 rounds on ZWAANHOEK and Targets in the marsh.	
	22nd.		Situation Normal - Nothing to report.	

For D.T.M.O. 49th (W.R.) Division.

Captain. R.F.A.

Army Form C. 2118.

WAR DIARY
or
INTELLIGENCE SUMMARY

(Erase heading not required.)   Page 4.

Instructions regarding War Diaries and Intelligence Summaries are contained in F.S. Regs., Part II. and the Staff Manual respectively. Title Pages will be prepared in manuscript.

Place	Date	Hour	Summary of Events and Information	Remarks and references to Appendices
GELUVELT SECTOR.	23rd.		Situation very quiet at all positions. The remaining two Mortars of Y/49 T.M.B. have now been put in action.	
	24th.		Nothing to report - Very quiet round positions.	
	25th.		A few shells fell near position at J.4.b.90.16 otherwise nothing to report.	
	26th.		Quiet day. - S.O.S. observed on our left from PASSCHENDAELE to the left of the ZONNEBEEK BROODSEINDE Road. Considerable difficulty is being experienced in keeping Dug-outs dry as in spite of continually pumping these fill to a depth of 2 to 3 feet every night.	
	27th.		Nothing to report - Enemy activity normal.	
	28th.		Nothing to report.- Situation round positions very quiet.	
	29th.		Normal enemy activity - No shells in the vicinity of the positions.	
	30th.		Quiet Day. - Nothing to report.	
	31st.		Nothing to report.	

R H Flanders
Captain R.F.A.
D.T.M.O. 49th (W.R.) Division.

49th Divisional Artillery.

49th DIVISIONAL TRENCH MORTARS

APRIL 1918.

WAR DIARY 49th Division Trench Mortars Army Form C. 2118.

or

INTELLIGENCE SUMMARY. Batteries 917

April 1918.

(Erase heading not required.)

Place	Date	Hour	Summary of Events and Information	Remarks and references to Appendices
			Ref. map Sheet 28.	
CHEUVELT SECTOR.	April 1st		Normal Activity. Nothing to report.	
	2nd		X/49 Battery moved to TOR TOP and took over mortars on the line from 39th Division Trench mortars who relieved them in the 49 Division Sector.	
	3rd		Nothing to report. Normal activity.	
	4th		do	
	5th		do	
	6th		do	
	7th		One Battery of 49 Div. Trench mortar Batteries man the mortars in the 6" Division Sector for the 6" Division who are short of personnel. Very little activity. Slight shelling near Dug-outs at TOR TOP.	
	8		Nothing to report.	
	9		do	
	10		Mortars still manned on both 6" & 49 Division fronts.	
	11		18 rounds fired on 49 Division front during the day.	
	12		19 rounds fired on various targets during the day.	

Nothing is fired for days 9&10

DTMO 49 Division.

Army Form C. 2118.

WAR DIARY
or
INTELLIGENCE SUMMARY.   Page 2.
(Erase heading not required.)

April 1918.

Place	Date	Hour	Summary of Events and Information	Remarks and references to Appendices
GHELUVELT SECTOR.	April 13	Ref. Map. Sheet. 28.	Slight activity - 21 rounds fired on various targets.	
	14th		Instructions received that as all 6" mortars T.M. Ammunition is required for use on this Army front - mortars in this Sector will be fired only for defensive purposes.	
	15th		In accordance with instructions received from 49 Divisional Arty. H.Q. Ammunition at the guns (100 rds) replenished and mortars withdrawn to the Army line during the night.	
	16th		Two mortars emplaced in the Army line and manned - Enemy has not yet followed up our evacuation.	
	17th		Nothing to report.	
	18th		Headquarters 49 Division T.M. Batteries moved to SYNDIKEBOOM CAMP (H.10.c.1.1.)	
	19th		Nothing to report.	
	20th		Enemy has not yet established his line in this Sector although reconnoitring parties have been seen.	

A. Lloyd Lieut for Capt R.F.A
DTMO 49 Division.

Army Form C. 2118.

WAR DIARY
or
INTELLIGENCE SUMMARY.
(Erase heading not required.)

Page 3.
April 1918.

Place	Date	Hour	Summary of Events and Information	Remarks and references to Appendices
CHELWELT SECTOR	April 21		Ref: Map. Sheet 28. Slight Artillery activity near position.	
	22		Enemy has not yet established line on this front.	
	23		Nothing to report	
	24		do.	
	25		20 men attached to Field Battery until reinforcements can be obtained — 15 men attached 19" D.a.C. for work on Dump.	
	26		Enemy approached our line and occupied evacuated ground. All rounds on 3 of the positions was expended and mortars withdrawn from the line. One mortar still remains in action.	
	27		128 men of 19 Siei Trench Mortar Batteries are now nothing for the Field Batteries with the exception of one attachment in the line.	
	28		Nothing to report.	
	29			
	30		Headquarters and stores removed to G.15.b.1.4. All Officers and men with the exception of two complete detachments are at G.15. G.1.4.	

Confidential

War Diary
of
49th Bn. Canadian Infantry Battalion
for
Month of May 1916

Original

Army Form C. 2118.

WAR DIARY
or
INTELLIGENCE SUMMARY.
(Erase heading not required.)

Place	Date	Hour	Summary of Events and Information	Remarks and references to Appendices
YPRES SECTOR	May 1st to 31st		49th (West Riding) Division Trench Mortar Batteries R.F.A. All Officers and men have been attached to Field Batteries and D.A.C during the whole of the month. No mortars have been in action. B/Walker Captain 18th Divisional Trench Mortar Officer 49th (W.R.) Division	

War Diary Vol 19
29th French Mortar Batteries
for
month of June 1918

Army Form C. 2118.

WAR DIARY
or
INTELLIGENCE SUMMARY.
(Erase heading not required.)

Place	Date	Hour	Summary of Events and Information	Remarks and references to Appendices
			49th Divisional Trench Mortar Batteries R.A.	
			June 1918.	
			Ref. map Belgium sheet 28 N.W. 1/20,000.	
YPRES SECTOR.	June 1st 22nd		All personnel of H.Q. Divisional Trench Mortar Batteries still employed with Field Batteries and D.A.C.	
	23rd		All Officers and Other Ranks recalled from Batteries and reformed. Location of Billets H.24.c.7.9.	
	4th		H.Q. Division T.M.B. Batteries relieved in the line by 1/49 T.M.B. 8 mortars in forward and 4 in reserve positions taken over together with 610 rounds Ammunition. Positions of mortars as follows:—	

AW Walker Capt RFA
DTMO 49 Division

Army Form C. 2118.

WAR DIARY
or
INTELLIGENCE SUMMARY. Sheet II
(Erase heading not required.)

Place	Date	Hour	Summary of Events and Information	Remarks and references to Appendices
YPRES SECTOR.	4th		1 mortar at I.4.a.#.3 1 mortar at I.8.d.10.55	
			" " I.3.d.40.42 1 " " I.8.d.05.47	
			1 " " I.9.c.67.32. 1 " " I.14.a.38.60	
			1 " " I.9.c.69.38. 1 " " I.14.a.46.49	
			2 " " H.11.b.80.15 2 " " H.11.b.85.45	
	5th		2nd Lieut. W.E. Benham and 2nd Lt. W.D.M. Warren joined from D.A.C. and posted to 4/49 T.M.B. 15 Reinforcements received from D.A.C.	
	6th to 26th		All mortars in the line have been manned continuously during this period but are only to be used to S.O.S. purposes. No S.O.S. has been sent up on this front during the period and all mortars have remained silent.	

OWalley Capt RFA
DTMO 49th Division.

Army Form C. 2118.

WAR DIARY
or
INTELLIGENCE SUMMARY.   SHEET III
(Erase heading not required.)

Instructions regarding War Diaries and Intelligence Summaries are contained in F. S. Regs., Part II. and the Staff Manual respectively. Title pages will be prepared in manuscript.

Place	Date	Hour	Summary of Events and Information	Remarks and references to Appendices
YPRES SECTOR.	June 1917			
	28		40 Rounds were fired from Mortar at I.4.a.40.30 on to MILL COTT in support of a raid. No hostile retaliation.	
			2 rounds registration fired from Mortar at I.4.a.40.30 enemy retaliated with about 20 H.V. shells round position.	
		11.30pm	40 rounds fired from Mortar at I.4.a.40.30 onto MILL COTT in support of a raid by 146th Infantry Brigade. Enemy Artillery was very active during the day in the vicinity of YPRES.	
	29.		Slight hostile Artillery activity on H.C.E. otherwise nothing to report.	
	30.		nothing to report. Ammunition Expended Casualties 82 rnds. nil.	

Rickier Capt R.F.A.
D.T.M.O 49 & Division

Vol 20

Confidential.

WAR DIARY
of
49th (W.R.) Division (Medium) Trench Mortar Batteries.
for July 1918.

Army Form C. 2118.

WAR DIARY
or
INTELLIGENCE SUMMARY.
(Erase heading not required.)

Instructions regarding War Diaries and Intelligence Summaries are contained in F.S. Regs., Part II. and the Staff Manual respectively. Title pages will be prepared in manuscript.

Place	Date	Hour	Summary of Events and Information	Remarks and references to Appendices
YPRES SECTOR.			49th Divisional Trench mortar Batteries R.A. July 1917	
			Ref. Map. Sheet 28. 1/40,000.	
	July 1st		49th Divisional Trench mortar Batteries are still manning 12 mortars on the YPRES front for defensive purposes — Two mortars only being at present within range of the enemy line.	
	2nd and 3rd		Mortars manned — Situation on this front quiet.	
	4th		A shoot was carried out from the forward mortars for the purpose of ascertaining whether charges had been effected by the damp. 20 rounds were fired with bombs that had been charged 6 weeks; no deterioration was found. 3 or 4 dug-outs and a trench were hit. A front line was hit and a large fire started.	

R.W. Walker Capt. R.F.A.
DTMO 49th Division.

WAR DIARY or INTELLIGENCE SUMMARY

Army Form C. 2118.

July 1917 Sheet II

Place	Date	Hour	Summary of Events and Information	Remarks and references to Appendices
YPRES SECTOR	July 9th 10th		No firing has been done during this period - mortars have been cleaned and general work carried out.	
	11th		At the request of the Infantry the following targets have been engaged. C.5.a.70.80 - 15 rounds - C.5.6.20.10 - 15 rounds -	
	12		A special demonstration has today been held at the Second Army Trench Mortar School, the DTMO of each Division in the Second Army being present.	
	19th 20th		Guns have been manned as usual - no firing has been done during this period.	
	21st		1 Officer (2nd Lt Heaton) and # O.R. proceeded to Second Army T.M. School for course.	
	22nd		Nothing to report.	
	23rd	11.30 am	15 rounds fired on Enemy Machine Gun Post at I.5.a.30.80 with good results. One mortar was withdrawn from reserve position at GOLDFISH CHATEAU and delivered to the # Touray Boy R.E. to be fitted with railway mounting.	

Rob Allen Capt RFA
DTMO 49 Division

WAR DIARY or INTELLIGENCE SUMMARY.

Army Form C. 2118.

SHEET. III

July 1918.

(Erase heading not required.)

Instructions regarding War Diaries and Intelligence Summaries are contained in F. S. Regs., Part II, and the Staff Manual respectively. Title pages will be prepared in manuscript.

Place	Date	Hour	Summary of Events and Information	Remarks and references to Appendices
YPRES SECTOR.	July 24th to 26th		Nothing to report - guns have been manned continuously - no firing has been done.	
	27th		One mortar has been emplaced in new position at I.9.d.76.73 and registered with 10 rds on RIFLE FARM.	
	28th		10 rounds registration fired from mortar at I.4.a.57-47. Nothing to report.	
	29th			
	30th		A shoot of 15 rounds was carried out on RIFLE FARM. 10 rounds fired with delay fuze at 12-30 a.m. and 20 rds a day & 6 incendiary rounds at 1 a.m. Machine Guns co-operated. The shooting was reported as good by a patrol sent out to report on same.	
	31st		20 rounds fired at Enemy T.M.s in I.5.b.17.27 and I.5.b.45.98. Firing was erratic, no direct hits being observed.	

Ammunition Expended. 120 rounds Casualties. Nil

A.F. Welch Capt R.F.A.
DTMO HQ 2nd (WR) Division.

Vol 21

War Diary
of
49th Division Medium Trench Mortar Batteries
for
August 1918.

Army Form C. 2118.

WAR DIARY
or
INTELLIGENCE SUMMARY.
(Erase heading not required.)

Instructions regarding War Diaries and Intelligence Summaries are contained in F. S. Regs., Part II. and the Staff Manual respectively. Title pages will be prepared in manuscript.

Place	Date	Hour	Summary of Events and Information	Remarks and references to Appendices
			#49: Divisional Trench Mortar Batteries R.A.	
			August 1918	
			R/Maps: Sheet 28 No,000	
YPRES SECTOR.	August 1st.		49. D.T.M. Batteries are still manning guns in the YPRES Sector newly being carried out weekly. 10 Rounds fired on Railway Crossing at I.10.a.99.75. 5 Rounds on RIFLE FARM.	
do.	2nd.		Two new positions have been built at I.1.d.6.3. No firing has been done today.	
do.	3rd.		No firing. General unrest on Eretaine.	
do.	4th.	8pm	20 rounds fired at enemy on Infantry on outpost at I.5.a.60.30 with good results. 12 rnds on Trench Junction at I.5.s.15.10.	
do.		7.30pm	10 rds on WEST FARM - 2 direct hits obtained. 10 rounds of 4-2 in retaliation fell about 300 yds in front of our front line.	

PMWalker
Lieut RFA
D.T.M.O. 49th (WR) Division

WAR DIARY or INTELLIGENCE SUMMARY

Army Form C. 2118.

49th Div. T.M. Battery.
Sheet II.   August 1918.

Place	Date	Hour	Summary of Events and Information	Remarks and references to Appendices
YPRES SECTOR Ref map Sheet 28 1/40,000	Aug. 5.	3-30 pm	10 Rounds were fired to test a Railway mounting for 6" Newton T.M. The mounting obviously firing prematurely took an ad aft tilt there is no more during firing. 2 rounds fired with 20° charge fell within bursts for line and Rfleet to range. all the firing was done at high angles (59° - 76°) owing to the revolved space the Low Browning was fired with a trailer attached to the mounting which enabled us to fire our last round and get clear within one second. Further tests will be carried out later. Firing from NEW Chateau Murtar. 5 rm on RIFLE FARM (I.10.a 90.50) 15 m on Railway Cutting (I.11.c 30.90) no retaliation.	
		11-30am 5-30pm	Mortars registered on CHUMP FARM with 14 rounds. At Infantry request fired on enemy outpost I.5.a. 52-13 - 18 rounds. Results Good.	
		6-15pm to 7pm	9 Rounds from white Chateau on Railway Cutting I.11.c.30.90. Observation - Good. Enemy retaliation - 2 rounds on front line at I.10.a.60.60.	

RWWalker Capt RFA
5TMO 49th (WR) Division

WAR DIARY 49th Division T.M. Battery

Army Form C. 2118.

INTELLIGENCE SUMMARY

Sheet III — August 1918

Place	Date	Hour	Summary of Events and Information	Remarks and references to Appendices
YPRES SECTOR Ref. map. Sheet 28 1/40,000	August 6th	11.30 a.m.	Fired 3 rounds on Enemy outpost at I.5.a.52.13 and 18 rounds on dugout at I.5.a.45.25. At request of G.O.C. 147 Infantry Brigade a new position was started at I.15.a.25-34. Zero line to run through HELLBLAST CORNER	
	7th		Nothing to report	
	8th		At request of Infantry 20 rounds fired on I.10.a.40.95. Several direct hits obtained.	
	9th		28 rounds fired on Outpost and dug-outs in vicinity of I.5.a.52.15. Outpost was hit 7 times. 11 rounds fired on Camouflage at I.5.c.65.80	
	10th		Nothing to report	
	11th		80 rounds fired in connection with operations by the Belgian Division on the left at 3.30 am	
	12th 13th 14th 15th		No firing has been done. Normal enemy activity.	

R Walker Capt RFA
DTMO 49 Division

WAR DIARY 49th Division T.M. Batteries

Army Form C. 2118.

INTELLIGENCE SUMMARY. Sheet IV August 1918.

(Erase heading not required.)

Place	Date	Hour	Summary of Events and Information	Remarks and references to Appendices
YPRES SECTOR	Aug 16.		Fired 61 rounds on wire in front of CAMBRIDGE ROAD between I.5.c.2.5c.b and I.5.a. 4.8.20. Several rounds were observed to fall on spots indicated by Intelligence Officer. 146 Brigade did during the night of the grass on wire cried by men.	
"	17.		Nothing to report.	
"	18.		do.	
"	19.		do.	
"	20. 11am		10 rounds fired from Light Railway at I.H.a. 05.05 on DULLY FARM I.5.c. 25.00	
"	21st		49th Divl. T.M. Batteries were relieved in the line by 34th Bn. T.M. Batteries 49th Divl T.M. Batteries withdrawn to billets in the HAANDEKOT Artillery Area (HAZEBROUCK. 2.H.39.54.) when 12 guns and 24 rds. Boxes over from 34th Division.	
HAANDEKOT.	22nd to 25th		Personnel of X/49 & Y/49 T.M.B. resting in billets in HAANDEKOT area.	

R.M.Walker Capt RFA
DTMO 49th Division

WAR DIARY 49th Division T.M. Battery Army Form C. 2118.

INTELLIGENCE SUMMARY. Sheet V August 1918

Instructions regarding War Diaries and Intelligence Summaries are contained in F. S. Regs., Part II. and the Staff Manual respectively. Title pages will be prepared in manuscript.

(Erase heading not required.)

Place	Date	Hour	Summary of Events and Information	Remarks and references to Appendices
EBBLINGHAM Ref. Map. HAZEBROUCK 5A 1/100,000.	Aug 26		Battery moved by lorry and billets for the night at EBBLINGHAM (4.E.90.83).	
AMETTES Ref. Map. HAZEBROUCK 5A 1/100,000	27	4pm	Moved by lorry from EBBLINGHAM to AMETTES (6.E.72.31). Under orders from Sixth 49 Division again moved to RAMECOURT (ferns 11. 2.D 75.45) and lorries returned to their unit.	
RAMECOURT Ref. Map.	28th to 3/um		On arrival at RAMECOURT (2.D 75.45). Gun Drill, Gas Drill etc carried out.	
LENS. 11 1/10,000.			Casualties during month nil.	
			Ammunition Expended. 382 rounds 6" newton.	

O/C Watch Cap RFA
DTMO 49 Division.

WR 22

Confidential.
War Diary
4ᵗʰ Division Trench Mortar Batteries
September 1918.

Army Form C. 2118.

WAR DIARY
or
INTELLIGENCE SUMMARY.

(Erase heading not required.)

Sheet 1

HQ. Divisional Trench Mortar Batteries RA
49th Division
for the month of September 1918.

Place	Date	Hour	Summary of Events and Information	Remarks and references to Appendices
RAMECOURT. 2.D.80.40.	1st		Ref Map Lens 11. 1/100.000. HQ. Divisional Trench Mortar Batteries RA moved by lorry from RAMECOURT to relieve an FREVIN CAPELLE (Ref 2D.80.40.) in billets at FREVIN CAPELLE. Arms Drill, and Drill Lectures and Recreational training carried out.	
FREVIN CAPELLE 2.H.70.25.	2nd to 5th 6th		60 men of their Batteries proceeded to be attached to the HQ (BVR) R.A.C. for the purpose of clearing up the salvage of ammunition in the FAMPOUX Area. Instructions received from C.R.A. 49 Division that 49 Division is 1st Army Reserve and ready to move at 12 hours notice.	
	8th to 12		Training as above too been proceeded with for the Several men remaining with the Batteries.	

R. Napier Capt RFA
A/DTMO 49th Division

WAR DIARY or INTELLIGENCE SUMMARY

Army Form C. 2118.

Sheet II
49 Div 6 Inch Mortar Battery
September 1918

Place	Date	Hour	Summary of Events and Information	Remarks and references to Appendices
FREVIN CAPELLE I.H.70.25.	Sept 13		Personnel at FREVIN CAPELLE moved by lorry under orders of 0.C./149 Bureau to Billets at H.L.C.3.5. By map was still firing. Guns and Postions on the line taken over from DTMO 4th Division as follows:—	

Postions (Forward)

No. 1. I. 20. b. 65.90.   Zero Line 70°
No. 2. I. 20. d. 65.90.   "   "   53°
No. 3. I. 14. a. 55.05.   "   "   78°-30'
No. 4. I. 14. a. 28.20.   "   "   77°

Postions (Rear)

No. 1. I. 19. d. 18.60.   Zero Line 90°
No. 2. I. 19. d. 18.60.   "   "   78°
No. 3. I. 7. a. 30.23.   "   "   56°-30'
No. 4. I. 7. a. 30.30.   "   "

5. I. 14. a. 18.62.   35°
6. I. 14. a. 10.90.   70°
7. I. 7. d. 40.53.   58°-30'
8. I. 7. d. 42.58.   52°-30'

92 men were withdrawn from H.Q. O.A.C. the remaining 28 being employed on the ammunition filling dump. Detachments on the line of 51st Division were relieved by personnel of this Battery. Relief completed by 4 am.

These Postions are only intended for S.O.S purposes being out of range for normal retaliation work.

R. Daysield
Major
9/DTO10 49 Division

WAR DIARY or INTELLIGENCE SUMMARY.

Army Form C. 2118.

Sheet II
49th Division T.M. Batteries
September 1918

Place	Date	Hour	Summary of Events and Information	Remarks and references to Appendices
Billets at H.Q. at Map Sheet 51 c. and positions in the line	Sept 13, 14 to 22nd	Ref maps Sheet 51 c. 1/40,000 & Sheet 51 B 1/40,000	Nothing in the line have been marred by day and by night. Positions have been cleaned up and improvements carried out. No S.O.S. has been received and no firing done.	
	22nd		49th Div. T.M.B's were relieved by 51st Division T.M.B's. Relief completed by 6pm and 49th Division T.M.B's proceeded by lorry and rails from CRA 49 Division to Billets in BRANDT CAMP. BRFY F14 b.5.5. ref map Sheet 51.c. 1/40,000 28 men from the A.R.P. rejoined the Batteries to day.	
BRFY B/Map Sheet 51 c. F.14 b.5.5	24		General training carried out.	
	25			
	26"		A 6" newton T.M. mounted on a lorry was to day given a trial. 7 rounds were fired. The lorry standing, the firing was satisfactory. A new hanging pin made to the design of the 5 Canadian Division was also tested with 2 rounds and proved fairly accurate. The upgoing guns slightly more so. We both know the other whom front used to twentieth further trials will be carried.	

R Blakeney
Capt RDTMO 49 Division
6 Oct 1917

A/DTMO 49 Division

WAR DIARY
INTELLIGENCE SUMMARY.

Sheet IV
49 Div T.M. Batteries
September 1918.

Place	Date	Hour	Summary of Events and Information	Remarks and references to Appendices
BRAY.	26 to 30.	Ref map Sheet 51c 1/40,000	Batteries are still under 12 hours notice to move. Nothing of note as occurred during the period. Recreational & General Training has been carried out. Ammunition Expended during the month. Nil Casualties during the month. nil. R Tupis Captain RFA A/D.T.M.O. 49 (WR) Division.	

War Diary

4⁰ Divisional Trench
Mortar Batteries.

for the month of October 1916

WAR DIARY
or
INTELLIGENCE SUMMARY.
(Erase heading not required.)

Army Form C. 2118.

49th Divisional Trench Mortar Batteries R.A.
49th Division
For the month of October 1918.

Place	Date	Hour	Summary of Events and Information	Remarks and references to Appendices
Reference Map LENS 11 1/100,000				
BRANDT CAMP LENS 21.29.13	1st to 9th		General training was carried out. Practice with new 6" Trench Mortar Bed. Lectures on German Light Trench Mortars were given and men instructed how to use same in the event of captures from the enemy. Physical training was given each day.	R.M.A.
CHERISY LENS 44.K.92.77	9th		Moved by Road to CHERISY (4.K.92.77) X Battery being attached to No.2 Section 49th D.A.C. and Y Battery to No.1 Section 49th D.A.C. for the move.	R.M.A.
Reference Map VALENCIENNES 1/100,000	10th		Moved to Billets in CAMBRAI at 44.C.60.12 and on arrival	R.M.A.

D.M.Maynder Capt R.A.
a/D.T.M.O 49 Division

Army Form C. 2118.

WAR DIARY
or
INTELLIGENCE SUMMARY.
(Erase heading not required.)

49th Divisional T.M. Batteries

October 1918

Ref map VALENCIENNES 1/100,000

Place	Date	Hour	Summary of Events and Information	Remarks and references to Appendices
Billets at 40 b 60.12	10th month		7 Officers and 60 other ranks of these Batteries proceeded to the attached to 245 and 246 Brigades R.F.A. for duty 5 other ranks proceeded for duty at Ammunition Refilling Point. 2 detachments were standing to in case the 2" – 6" Trench Mortars which were mounted on Lorries should be required. Remainder were attached to Sections 49th D.A.C. for duty.	RMA RMA RMA
ESCHDOEUVRES 4D 25. 35	12th		Moved to Billets in ESCHDOEUVRES at 4D.25.35.	
NAVES. 4D 42.78	23rd		Moved to Billets in NAVES at 4D 42.78	
	25th		2" – 6" Trench Mortar Beds mounted on Trench G.S. Wagon Wheels and Axle received – fully tried and reported on as satisfactory with a suggestion that the iron horn which form the Trail should be made stronger as an improvement.	RMA

RM Newylds
A/D.T.M.O 49 Division

Capt 1.7.0
49 Division

WAR DIARY
or
INTELLIGENCE SUMMARY.
(Erase heading not required.)

Army Form C. 2118.

49th Divisional T.M. Batteries
October 1918.

Place	Date	Hour	Summary of Events and Information	Remarks and references to Appendices
Billets at 3E.77&4	28th		Ref. Map VALENCIENNES 1/100,000. Moved to Billets near DENAIN at 3E.77.84. All other ranks with the exception of 3 signallers & called from 246 Brigade R.F.A. and proceeded for duty on Ammunition Refilling Point.	RNA
	31st		A course on 77mm German gun was given at A/245 Major Lines. All T.M. personnel attached to that Brigade attended. 2 detachments consisting of 1 officer and 9 other ranks each were detailed by Division to move forward with the infantry in the attack commencing 1-11-18 with a view to using 77mm guns captured from the enemy.	RNA
			Ammunition expended during month NIL. Casualties during month 1 Officer & other Ranks.	RNA

RM Kennedy Capt RFA
O/C D.T.M.O 49th Division

Army Form C. 2118.

WAR DIARY
or
INTELLIGENCE SUMMARY.
(Erase heading not required.)

49th Divisional T.M. Batteries
October 1918

Instructions regarding War Diaries and Intelligence Summaries are contained in F. S. Regs., Part II. and the Staff Manual respectively. Title pages will be prepared in manuscript.

Place	Date	Hour	Summary of Events and Information	Remarks and references to Appendices
Billets Ref map VALENCIENNES 1/100,000 4 c 60.12	10th		7 Officers and 60 other ranks of these Batteries proceeded to be attached to 245 and 246 Brigades R.F.A. for duty. 5 other ranks proceeded for duty at Ammunition Refilling Point. 2 detachments were standing to in case the 2"-6" Trench Mortars which were wounded on lorries should be required. Remainder were attached to Sections 49th D.A.C. for duty.	RMM RMM RMM
ESCHADOEUVRES 4D.25.35.	12th		Moved to Billets in ESCHADOEUVRES at 4D.25.35.	
NAVES. 4D 42.78	23rd		Moved to Billets in NAVES at 4D 42.78	RMM
	25th		2"-6" Trench Mortar Beds mounted on Front G.S. Wagon Wheels and axle received - fully tested and reported on as satisfactory with a suggestion that the iron bars which form the frame should be made stronger as an improvement.	

RMReynolds
Capt. 1/5.
O/C D.T.M.O. 49 Division

T.131. Wt. W08-776. 500,000. 4/15. Sir J.C. & S.

WAR DIARY or INTELLIGENCE SUMMARY

Army Form C. 2118.

49th Divisional T.M. Batteries

October 1918.

Ref Map. VALENCIENNES 1/100.000

Place	Date	Hour	Summary of Events and Information	Remarks and references to Appendices
Billets at 3.E.77 & 28			Moved to Billets near DENAIN at 3.E.77.S8. All other ranks with the exception of 3 signallers recalled from 246 Brigade R.F.A. and proceeded for duty on Ammunition Refilling Point.	RMA
	30th		A course on 77mm German gun was given at A/245 Major Lines. All T.M. personnel attended to that Brigade attended. 2 detachments consisting of 1 Officer and 9 other ranks each were detailed by Division to move forward with the infantry in the attack commencing 1.11.18 with a view to using 77mm guns captured from the enemy. Ammunition expended during month NIL.	RMA
			Casualties during month 1 Officer 3 other ranks.	RMA

RM Kennedy Capt. R.F.A.
D.T.M.O. 49th Division

WAR DIARY
or
INTELLIGENCE SUMMARY.

Army Form C. 2118.

49th Divisional Trench Mortar Batteries
H.Q. Quiévy
For the month of November 1918

Place	Date	Hour	Summary of Events and Information	Remarks and references to Appendices
Reference Map VALENCIENNES 1/100,000 Sheet at 3E.17.S4.				
			D.T.M.O. with No 1 Section 49th Bde in billets at 3.E.17.S4. DENAIN. Officers, N.C.O. and men of the 49th Div. Trench Mortar Batteries attached to 245th Bde R.F.A., 246 Bde R.F.A. and 49 D.A.C. for duty. When trench mortar work is ordered, returned to recalled from these attachments.	R.O.
	1st		In accordance with orders received from 49th Division yesterday 2 detachments consisting of 1 officer and 9 other ranks per detachment moved forward with the infantry in attack launched this morning with the object of raising 77 m.m. guns in the event of any captured from the enemy.	A.O.

A/D.T.M.O. 49 Div
Major RA

WAR DIARY
or
INTELLIGENCE SUMMARY.

Army Form C. 2118.

49th Divisional Trench Mortar Batteries
November 1918

(Erase heading not required.)

Instructions regarding War Diaries and Intelligence Summaries are contained in F.S. Regs., Part II. and the Staff Manual respectively. Title pages will be prepared in manuscript.

Place	Date	Hour	Summary of Events and Information	Remarks and references to Appendices
			Ref. Map VALENCIENNES 1/100.000	
Willetts J.F. 77. b. 2.7 5.5.	9th Cont.		Lowest mere captures. Nothing to report.	R₁/
Willetts 2.G.31.13 VALENCIENNES	10th		Moved to Willetts at 2.G.31.13 near VALENCIENNES. Nothing to report.	R₂/ R₂A
ERQUENNES 2.J.S1.31	9th 10th 11th 12th		Moved to ERQUENNES 2.J.S1.31. Hostilities closed the day at 1100 hours. Nothing to report. Officers, NCOs and men still attached to 245-246 Brigade R.F.A.	R₂ R₂A
MARLY 2.G.S.2 MASTAING 3.D.65.61	29th 28th 29th 30th		Proceeded by road to MARLY 2.G.S.2 Continued march to MASTAING 3.D.65.61 Arrived at destination in area N.E. of DOUAI	R₃/ R₃A R₃/ R₃/

R. Maguid Captain R.F.A.
a/D.T.M.O. 49th Division

Army Form C. 2118.

49 DTM By

WAR DIARY
OF
INTELLIGENCE SUMMARY.
(Erase heading not required.)

Instructions regarding War Diaries and Intelligence Summaries are contained in F.S. Regs., Part II. and the Staff Manual respectively. Title pages will be prepared in manuscript.

WO 95 2 5

Place	Date	Hour	Summary of Events and Information	Remarks and references to Appendices

Reference Map 1/100,000

49th Divisional Trench Mortar Batteries
49th Division
For the month of December 1918.

VALENCIENNES

1st D.T.M.O. with No 1 Section 49th (With) D.A.C. at 1 By 43.05
31st X-Y/49 Trench Mortar Batteries attached to 245, 246 Brigades R.F.A.
and 49th D.A.C.

Nothing to report.

N. Rogers, Capt. R.F.A. (T)
D.T.M.O. 49th Division

www.ingramcontent.com/pod-product-compliance
Lightning Source LLC
Chambersburg PA
CBHW081531160426
43191CB00011B/1739